ANGELINA
JOLIE

ANGELINA JOLIE

KATHLEEN TRACY

ECW PRESS

The publication of *Angelina Jolie* has been generously supported
by the Government of Canada through the
Book Publishing Industry Development Program.

CANADIAN CATALOGUING IN PUBLICATION DATA
Tracy, Kathleen
Angelina Jolie
Includes bibliographical references.
ISBN 1-55022-441-7

1. Jolie, Angelina, 1975- .
2. Motion picture actors and actresses – United States – Biography.
I. Title.
PN2287.J64T72 2001   781.43'028'92   C00-932377-5

Front cover photo by George Holz / Outline.
Back cover photo by J. Dunas / Sygma / MAGMA.
Copyedited by Mary Williams.
Cover and interior design by Guylaine Régimbald – SOLO DESIGN.
Typesetting by Yolande Martel.
This book is set in Electra and Trajan.

Printed by Printcrafters, Inc., Winnipeg, Manitoba, Canada.

Distributed in Canada by General Distribution Services,
325 Humber College Boulevard, Etobicoke, Ontario M9W 7C3.

Distributed in the United States by LPC Group,
1436 West Randolph Street, Chicago, IL 60607, U.S.A.

Distributed in Europe by Turnaround Publisher Services, Unit 3,
Olympia Trading Estate, Coburg Road, Wood Green, London, N2Z 6T2.

Distributed in Australia and New Zealand by Wakefield Press,
17 Rundle Street (BOX 2266), Kent Town, South Australia 5071.

Published by ECW PRESS
Suite 200
2120 Queen Street East
Toronto, Ontario M4E 1E2.
ecwpress.com

CONTENTS

INTRODUCTION

In another era, Angelina Jolie would have been considered an eccentric. A natural beauty who dismisses her looks as uninspiring, Jolie can come across as painfully vulnerable. But she also radiates street smarts, and she's been known to taunt interviewers by telling them tales of self-mutilation with a glint in her eye. She will discuss her bisexual exploits openly, but she'll also maintain that she's a traditionalist at heart. The idea of settling down with the love of her life and having babies both attracts and intimidates her.

Jolie is definitely not your typical oldtime leading lady.

Yet she's one of the fastest-rising stars in Hollywood. The daughter of Oscar-winner John Voight, Jolie has strong ties to the movie industry: both of her parents are actors, and her godmother is Jacqueline Bisset. Jolie is a movie star who seems genuinely indifferent to the attention she receives, but with each new role she takes on that attention intensifies. Though she hasn't been in the business long, she's already built a varied and impressive body of work; and now, set to star in the film *Tomb Raider*, Jolie is poised on the brink of superstardom. She'll soon ascend to the ranks of such people as Tom Cruise and Harrison Ford—actors who have managed to strike a successful career balance between roles that showcase their artistic craft and star turns in action-adventure blockbusters.

Angelina Jolie is definitely a leading lady of the future.

ONE

FAMILY BUSINESS

For as long as there has been a Hollywood, acting has been a family business. From such sibling combinations as the Marx brothers and the Baldwin brothers, to such parent-child pairings as Kirk and Michael Douglas and Janet Leigh and Jamie Lee Curtis, family connections abound. Those connections thrive on the technical side of the biz, as well—the children of grips, gaffers, designers, and stuntmen often follow in their parents' footsteps. All of this leads many people to believe that nepotism is rampant in Hollywood.

While the legendary Barrymores (considered America's first thespian dynasty), silent-screen sweethearts Dorothy and Lillian Gish, and lovely leading ladies Constance and Joan Bennett made no effort to conceal their family ties, many of their colleagues did—and still do. To avoid accusations of nepotism, or simply to avoid being perceived as trying to cash in on a famous name, a number of performers have renamed themselves. Here are just a few examples: sisters Olivia DeHavilland and Joan Fontaine; brothers James Arness and Peter Graves; siblings Shirley MacLaine and Warren Beatty (MacLaine uses an altered version of their mother's maiden name, and Beatty retains the family name).

The Hollywood film industry has embraced some particularly strong father-daughter units. John Huston (whose father was veteran character actor Walter Huston) and Angelica Houston spring to mind. So do Ryan O'Neal—who wasn't able to make the leap from leading man to middle-aged character actor—and Tatum O'Neal—whose career was derailed by a bad marriage and drugs.

These days, the most successful father-daughter act in Hollywood is likely Jon Voight and Angelina Jolie. Their story, a unique and intriguing one, seems to be dominated by two factors. First, Voight left the family when Angelina was a small child, and the two have only recently revived their relationship. Second, Angelina has entered her father's profession and in her work has displayed an emotional depth and complexity that occasionally border on creative madness.

It's one of those central human mysteries that a child who thoroughly rejects many of her parents' values and aspirations will ultimately come to share them. Perhaps there's something in the old cliché that the apple never falls very far from the tree—in Angelina Jolie's case, certainly not as far as it may have wanted.

By the time Angelina Jolie Voight was born, on June 4, 1975, her mother had already given up her acting career. Marcheline Bertrand had quit to raise James, then two. The children's father, however, was working harder than ever. Jon Voight had always been single-minded in his pursuits, even as a child growing up in Yonkers, a New York City suburb.

Jon was the son of Elmer Voight, a professional golfer, and Barbara, a housewife. At just eight years of age, Elmer, whose family had recently immigrated from Czechoslovakia, found work as a caddy. The members of the all-Jewish country club where he worked mentored him, teaching him not only about golf but also about table manners and the social graces; they taught him to speak English, as well. When Elmer became an adult, he never forgot the kindness these people had shown him, and he made a point of helping others whenever he could. He also made sure that his three sons did likewise, but he accomplished this by entertaining them, not by disciplining them. Every night, Elmer Voight would tell his sons Jon, Barry, and Chip funny stories that contained important moral lessons. Jon Voight described his dad to Eric Harrison of the *Los Angeles Times* as, "just a delightful man, a wonderful man, full of fun. And he had very strong principles. He didn't tolerate dishonesty, didn't like liars and didn't suffer fools gladly. People loved him."

Evidently, Elmer's approach to parenting had a positive effect. Barry grew up to be a geoscience professor at Penn State and one of the world's leading volcanologists. Chip—who goes by the name Chip Taylor—became a successful songwriter who penned the Troggs classic "Wild Thing." As a youngster, Jon showed a flair for both athletics and art. "He could have been a golf pro, or even an artist," Barry told *People*'s Larry Sutton. "He was the guy everyone called on to do all the serious drawings for the school yearbook, cartoons, even sets for the plays."

Jon, however, aspired to be an actor. So, after graduating from Washington DC's Catholic University, he moved to New York City, where he enrolled in acting classes and landed a few small acting jobs. For Voight, as for most young actors, money was tight. "I remember, one of the best restaurants that I ever went to in my life was a cafeteria on Forty-seventh Street near Eighth Avenue," he told journalist Prairie Miller in an online interview. "Because you could go into that place and for very, very little money you could get a lot of food! And it saved my life, it was a place I could eat! Continuously!"

In 1962, Voight fell in love with actress Lauri Peters, and they married. Voight was still only working sporadically, picking up odd jobs here and there, and the couple had to struggle to make ends meet. Fortunately, Voight admits, he could turn to Elmer for help: "I had a dad who took care of me. I used to borrow from my father." Being consistently supportive and understanding, Voight now realizes, "was difficult in a certain sense for a parent. Because you never know if a kid is going to be successful." But, he adds, "my dad saw me through it. And if I wasn't successful in that area, I probably would have moved to another area eventually. So his support was meaningful to me at that time."

So when Elmer Voight was struck by a car and killed in 1964, Jon was devastated. He went through an extended period of mourning, but rather than give up on his dream of becoming an actor, he continued to work towards it with renewed determination. He knew that Elmer would have wanted him to, so he kept going to auditions and taking any roles that came his way. Then suddenly, in 1969, Jon Voight became famous. In fact, he became infamous.

When director John Schlesinger's film *Midnight Cowboy* came out, it generated an enormous buzz. Everyone was talking about the film's shocking subject matter, as well as the stellar performances of its stars—Dustin Hoffman and Jon Voight. According to Voight, he'd heard they were casting *Midnight Cowboy*, which was based on a novel he'd read, and told his buddy Dustin Hoffman that he would be perfect as the conniving protagonist, Ratso Rizzo. He also saw himself in the role of Texan hayseed Joe Buck, who becomes a male prostitute in New York's sleazy Forty-second Street district. The two friends went after these juicy roles, but while Hoffman won the role of Rizzo, Voight had to wait to capture his prize. The film's producers cast a "name" actor as Buck, but he dropped out at the last minute. Voight was ready and willing to fill the void.

Midnight Cowboy would make Hollywood history as the first X-rated film to win the Oscar for Best Picture. Today such fare would only receive an R rating, but in the 1960s the story of a male prostitute who has a homoerotic relationship with his ad hoc pimp made people very nervous. The critics, however, had no qualms, and they sang *Midnight Cowboy*'s praises. Voight now had the entrée he needed: casting office doors opened wide to receive him.

Voight's marriage to Peters had fallen apart in 1967, so when he made the decision to relocate to Los Angeles he was on his own. He set himself up in Hollywood and was soon offered roles in a string of successful films, including *Deliverance*, *The Odessa File*, and *Catch-22*. Voight remarried as well—this time his bride was twenty-year-old French actress Marcheline Bertrand. In 1973, their son James Haven was born; and Angelina came along two years later. Marcheline and Jon gave their children middle names that could serve as last names because they foresaw the day that James and Angelina might want to pursue entertainment careers without trading on the Voight name.

Looking back, Jon recalls that even as a child Angelina showed signs of the kind of person she would grow up to be. "Everyone who has children knows that mysterious aspect," he commented to *USA Today*'s Jeannie Williams. "Before we program them to make our lives convenient." Voight added that his daughter, who he sometimes calls Jellybean, was "a very bright baby. She always had so much to say, even before she could talk!" He also claimed that the two of them share a reflective, philosophical nature.

Speaking to Larry Sutton of *People*, Voight described another of Angelina's compelling traits—her fierce independence. "Since she was a baby she wouldn't let you help her, even with her ABCs. She'd say, 'No! I do it! I do it!' That's the way she is." Apparently, young Angelina was also somewhat morbid and drawn to dark thoughts. In 1996, she herself told *People* that at one point she thought she would be a funeral director. "There's something about death that is comforting. The thought you could die tomorrow frees you to appreciate your life now." But to *Rolling Stone*'s Mimi Udovitch she remarked, "I've kind of discovered that if I think about death much more than some people [do], it's probably because I love life more than those people." Angelina believes that her views on the subject of death come out of personal experience. "My grandfather died when I was about nine, and I've— well, not always hated funerals, but I've always felt that they were so not a celebration of the life of the person, and that the crossing over could be a beautiful thing and a time of comfort where people could reach out to each other. And I think there's also just that it's a tradition."

Perhaps her father's absence during her formative years also contributed to Angelina's dark outlook. When she was still a toddler, Jon and Marcheline separated. Still only twenty-five years old, Bertrand found herself a single mom with two young children to raise. "He was the perfect example of an artist who couldn't be married," Jolie would tell *People* many years later. "He had the perfect family, but there's something for him that's very scary about that."

Marcheline pulled up stakes and went back to New York with the children. When they'd settled in, she began taking James and Angelina to the theater on a regular basis. Jolie has plenty of recollections from this period of her childhood but one of the most vivid was the time her mom inadvertently introduced her to knives. "I went to the Renaissance Fair with my mom when I was a little girl and there were all these kinda *knives*," she told talk show host Conan O'Brien. "There's something really beautiful and traditional about them—different countries have different weapons and blades and there's something beautiful about them to me. So I began collecting knives. I've collected weapons since I was a little girl."

When Jolie was eleven, Marcheline moved the family back to Los Angeles, making it easier for the children to see their dad—although Voight says he never saw the separation as an excuse to stop being a parent. "When Marcheline and I broke up," he says, "I made a solemn promise that I wouldn't let it interfere with my relationship with Angelina and her brother, Jamie. I said I'd try to see them as often as possible and that I'd always be there if they needed me."

At that age, while Angelina may have really needed a mom and a dad, what she seemed to need even more was a style consultant. Determined to display her individuality, she dyed her hair blue and wore studded jackets. "When we moved back from New York, I had gotten really into leather," she told Dany Jucaud of *Paris Match*. "I think I loved Michael Jackson or something. I used to wear the leather jackets with the zippers, or collars with studs on them, and I used to ask if I could go to school wearing studs."

In 1978, not long after he and Marcheline had separated, John Voight won the Best Actor Oscar for his portrayal of a paraplegic Vietnam veteran in the film *Coming Home*. Once again, it was a role the studio didn't initially want to offer him. Instead, the producers wanted to cast him as Jane Fonda's husband, a by-the-book military man (a role that eventually went to Bruce Dern). "I wasn't an A-list actor," Voight admitted to Louis Hobson of the *Ottawa Sun*. "But Jane Fonda wanted me for the lead. They only came back to me when every actor they approached turned them down. No big-name actor of the time wanted to risk his reputation." But, as Voight explained, after playing a male prostitute in *Midnight Cowboy*, "nothing worried me."

Despite his Oscar win, Voight continued to experience lean times—which were made leaner by the fact that he seemed incapable of hanging on to his money. He would spend it as soon as he earned it, never even buying himself a house.

As for Marcheline and the kids, when they moved back to L.A. they took up residence in what locals call the "slums" of Beverly Hills—several neighborhoods of apartment blocks adjacent to the famous district of high-priced homes. Jolie told Deanna Kizis of *Harper's Bazaar* that, based on her father's career status, people would make assumptions about her lifestyle. They failed to understand that Voight was "very uncomfortable about success. Like, somehow it was great to live without, to give away everything you had. You know, to have money meant that maybe you were a bad person or something. Everyone thought I had money. I had to go to my teacher and say, 'I can't keep redoing my papers because I don't have a computer.' And I

Angelina's freshman year
CLASSMATES.COM YEARBOOK ARCHIVES

remember the teacher saying, 'Have your father buy you one.'" While her Beverly Hills High School classmates threw their ample allowances around in Rodeo Drive boutiques, Jolie filled out her wardrobe by shopping at thrift stores and the gen-Xer shops on Melrose Avenue.

Voight knows that he wasn't the best financial provider for his children. "I went through some dramas," he confided to Prairie Miller. "I think as I look back, all of those times are of good use to me, because they taught me many things. And maybe taught my kids a few things as well. When they saw me struggle with different things, and all the real difficulties that I've had, if I shared them, they'd become lessons for them as well. So they can see, well, this happened here, and this is the way that Dad responded to it. And if they know my weaknesses as well as my strengths, that doesn't hurt either." Whatever embarrassment she may have suffered early on, Jolie now takes a pragmatic approach to her dad's foibles. "There's one thing I can say about him: Not once did we lack for anything. And he spent all his spare time with us. If he couldn't see us, we'd call."

When she was seven, Angelina made her screen debut in director

Hal Ashby's *Lookin' to Get Out*. Voight starred in, and cowrote, this offbeat comedy in which Jolie had a walk-on part. Her mom also appeared, billed as "girl in jeep." Although Ashby and Voight had created screen magic together in *Coming Home*, the title of *Lookin' to Get Out* describes the audience's reaction to the flick. By any standard, it was a complete flop. Not only did the critics skewer it, but it also bled red at the box office, costing seventeen million dollars to make and recouping only $300,000 in domestic ticket sales.

The one bright spot in all of this was the fact that *Lookin' to Get Out* confirmed something for Voight that he already suspected. His daughter had screen presence. "Looking back, there was evidence at a very early age that she would be an actor," Voight said to the *New York Post*. "She would take anything and make an event out of it. She was always very busy and creative and dramatic."

Jolie clearly remembers the thrill she experienced at the attention paid to her as a child performer. Speaking to Christine James of *Box Office* she joked, "I found that when I was four years old, there was this part of me that liked making people laugh and liked wearing glitter underwear. And how can you not?" In her *Rolling Stone* interview she recalled that she used to "wear costumes all the time. I had this black velvet frilly little showgirl thing with sparkles on my butt, and I used to love those plastic high heels. There's a picture of me having my five-year-old birthday party: I had curled my hair and put lipstick on—very girly."

In 1997, Jolie was interviewed by her dad for *Interview* magazine. In the course of that conversation, she talked about her early love of the spotlight and the source of the self-confidence she drew on when she performed. "God, my earliest memories are of my brother, Jamie—your son—pointing the home video camera at me and saying, 'C'mon, Ange, give us a show.' Neither you or Mom ever said, 'Be quiet! Stop talking!' I remember you looking me in the eye and asking, 'What are you thinking? What are you feeling?' That's what I do in my job now—I say, 'Okay, how do I feel about this?' And I immediately know, because that's how I grew up." Later Jolie told Louis Hobson of the *Calgary Sun*, "I loved some kind of expression. I didn't know what it was going to be. I didn't know if I could write it, or paint that well, but I knew I could feel it."

Angelina was marching to the beat of a different drummer in other areas of her life, as well. She has said that her first sexual fantasy involved *Star Trek*'s Mr. Spock. "I think a lot of women might agree with this," she commented to Jay Leno on a 1998 installment of *The Tonight Show*. "Because he's kinda reserved and he has that, like, sense of, 'You can't break through to me, and you can't touch me.' So he's a challenge, you know? You kinda think, 'Oh, I can get him.' There's got to be something underneath those ears and hair, and, yeah . . . it's kinda perverted." Maybe so, but the young Jolie was also intrigued by Vlad the Impaler.

It might not surprise many people to know that when Angelina was a kindergarten tyke she and some of her female classmates formed a gang called the Kissy Girls. Their purpose was to chase little boys, catch them, kiss them, and listen to them holler. Recalled Jolie to *Rolling Stone*'s Udovitch, "I had two good friends who became my boyfriends, and I think the school called my parents because we were in front of the school grabbing each other. Obviously that was disturbing to the parents and the people driving by."

Although Voight worked at maintaining a hands-on relationship with his children, the divorce still had a profound effect on Angelina and James. And each sibling reacted differently. Because Angelina and her father shared many personality traits, the two of them clashed most dramatically; this occurred during Angelina's adolescence. As Angelina herself acknowledged to *Movieline*, "We had a heavy relationship because we were so much alike." She would continue in this vein during a Beat Box Betty online interview: "He wasn't like a dad. He was this man I knew. He was a very complicated man and he always meant well and I always wanted to love him, but we both attacked each other because we both thought we were right about everything. We'd debate anything. But I love that. That's why I question everything. But I don't have a bad relationship with my dad. He wasn't there a lot, so I became strong for my mom."

Later, in an interview with Hobson, Jolie would reveal that one of the issues she had with Voight was the fact that he left her mom to manage alone when she and James were so young. "It's something that took me a very long time to come to terms with." She did, finally, come to terms with her father's decision, and the story makes for interesting interview material, particularly since both have achieved success in the same glamorous profession and gained a certain notoriety. But all of this tends to overshadow a simple truth of Angelina's existence. Marcheline Bertrand had far more influence over their daughter during her formative years than Voight did, through the simple power of maternal proximity.

While Marcheline did shuttle her children back and forth between New York and Los Angeles, the West Coast was their primary home. It was here that Angelina would begin to strike out on her own. She began modeling at fourteen. Her lanky body and exotic face made her a natural. At each step, Marcheline advised and protected her. She wanted to make sure that Angelina was treated appropriately by agents and photographers, so she assigned herself the task of acting as her daughter's manager. Jolie commented on the advantages of this arrangement: "She handles me with care and considers me a daughter first and model second." (Which, no doubt, is why Marcheline affectionately refers to Angelina as "Bunny.")

Voight, of course, did lend Jolie some professional support as well. Angelina said to *News Extra*, "He told me a long time ago: 'I don't know how much I can help you, but I'll do my best. Whatever knowledge I've gained, I'll willingly pass on to you.'" Even before Angelina had committed herself to pursuing an acting career, her famous father at times seemed intent on helping her to follow in his footsteps, if only because it would strengthen their bond. When Angelina would spend the occasional weekend with her dad, they'd go to the beach and catch up on each other's lives. Voight would frequently discuss potential movie projects with his daughter, asking her opinion and insisting that she was his best critic. He'd even decline roles she didn't approve of.

As Jolie and Voight worked out their problems in their own way, others assumed that Jolie was bottling up her feelings or subverting them. This infuriated her. She told Alison Boleyn of *Marie Claire*, "I was in school and you could get extra credit for going to a therapist. It was just a part of life studies, psychology. So I went. And I realized how dangerous these people could be. This person kept talking about my feelings for my father. I'd say, 'No, I'm not angry. I understand. I think my parents are both wonderful individuals.' And she just couldn't believe it wasn't a problem for me. I can remember coming in one day

Angelina's sophomore year
CLASSMATES.COM YEARBOOK ARCHIVES

and saying I had a dream and I totally lied. I said I dreamt that I
stabbed my father with a fork, and she said, 'Aha, I see.' And I thought,
'You fucking asshole.'" That was the end of therapy for Jolie. "Today if
I need to work things out I just drive a car around for a couple hours."

When the teenaged Angelina enrolled in the exclusive Lee Strasberg
Theater Institute, she may have been influenced to take that particular
course of action by her father. Or she may simply have been destined
to become an actress all along. She told Stephanie Mansfield of *USA
Weekend* that one of the first workshop performances she did at the
institute was from *Room Service*, the Marx Brothers movie. "There
were all these different roles in it, but I wanted to audition for the big,
mean manager. I was sixteen, and I thought I should play the role as
this German dominatrix." She went on to explain that Voight "came to
see this play to see what kind of an actor I was going to be or what kind
of choices I was going to be making. And instead of seeing me come
out as a sweet little girl or the sexy woman who's from out of town and
staying at the hotel, I came in as this insanely driven, dominant person

who everybody laughed at. That's when he realized, 'She does share my sense of the bizarre.'"

Even though she'd plunged into her professional training with such zest, Jolie backed off after a while. "I stopped acting and had some regular teenage years, so that I had a little more to build on when I went back," she said to Elizabeth Snead of *USA Today*. Her interest in acting didn't wane during this time. She started going over to her dad's house every Sunday. As Voight told Hobson in the *Ottawa Sun*, "We'd read plays together. Arthur Miller's *A View from the Bridge* is one of my favorite plays. I was overwhelmed. Her reading was as good as anyone who'd played the daughter part opposite me on stage. I knew right then and there she was going to be an actress."

Which is not necessarily to say that the idea of his daughter going into show business didn't occasionally give Voight pause. Jolie told Jack Garner of Gannett News Service, "My mother pointed me in certain directions and has always been supportive." Voight was initially more reserved. "He didn't want to send me off to do something unless it was something I really needed to do. He was worried that I was doing it just because I had grown up with it, and thought it would be easy. He knew it was a certain kind of a life, and hoped that I had what it would take to do it. He wanted me to fight it out, and prove it for myself."

When she was still sixteen, Angelina moved out of her mother's home and into a small, nearby studio. Intelligent and articulate, she'd graduated from high school a year and a half early, which freed her to explore her professional options full time. "I didn't know exactly what I wanted, but I knew I didn't know any other way to express me. My way of explaining things to people is through emotions—to listen to people and feel things. That's what an actor is, so I think that's why I had to do it." Like many fledgling actresses, Angelina turned to music videos as a way of gaining exposure and experience. She starred in videos for Lenny Kravitz and Meatloaf, driving to the auditions and the shoots in the Ford truck she'd bought with her modeling money.

James gave his little sister a hand, as well. As a film major at the University of Southern California he made five films for class projects, and he cast Angelina in every one of them. Angelina not only appreciated the opportunity to broaden her work experience, but she also enjoyed being around her brother. James was as conservative as Angelina

Angelina and her brother, James Haven

was wild, and the two had become best friends. Angelina felt she could talk to her brother about anything, and she loved his gentle side—he refused to swear, saying "gosh-darn frigging" instead of "goddamn fucking," the way she would.

Angelina always did things her own way, and she admired others who did the same. When something captured her interest she'd jump right in, attending a punk rock concert one day and taking ballroom dancing lessons the next. She was equally keen on undermining the perception that she was a Hollywood insider. How could she be, she reasoned, if her father, who was supposedly the provider of her insider credentials, was going through an extended career dry spell? This spell lasted through Jolie's late teens and early twenties, the period when she was getting into the business herself. "It's not like he really lived 'Hollywood' or had lots of money," she pointed out to Hobson in a *Calgary Sun* interview. "I grew up apart from it. He was in the past. He was an artist but not going to premieres."

Obviously very sensitive to the suggestion that she might exploit her family name to advance her career, Angelina now made the formal decision to drop the Voight moniker. On that issue, at least, Jon and Marcheline had been prescient. "I'm my mother and my father's child and I'm also my own person," Jolie declared to Bert Osborne of *Jezebel*. "From the very beginning, I didn't want to feel like I was walking into a room and automatically being compared to him, or feeling like I was being let into any rooms because of him." To Jeff Strickler of the *Minneapolis Star Tribune*, she added, "I don't want to be hired because of my name. I'm not ashamed of my background. I'm very proud of my father and the work he's done. But I don't want anyone to be expecting me to be him."

Not to worry. As soon as Angelina hit the big screen it was clear that no one would ever mistake her for Jon Voight. From the outset it was apparent that Angelina was a unique individual, both professionally and personally.

TWO

A CRASH COURSE ON LOVE

As she matured, Angelina's looks took on an exotic quality. She wasn't a classic beauty, particularly as defined by Hollywood. She was slender, with arms and legs that could almost be described as spindly; she was also buxom and had a head that seemed just a touch too large for her body. But Angelina's face, her full lips and wide smile, tantalized the camera lens. Jolie herself commented that she'd always felt as if she looked like a Muppet. And her favorite body part was her forearms—she liked the way her veins looked.

Jolie had another unusual distinguishing feature. When she was modeling, the camera seldom picked up the faint scar running along her left jawline. Although Jolie has never gone into great detail, she did acknowledge to Mimi Udovitch in *Esquire* that the scar was the result of a knife experiment she and a boyfriend conducted when she was fourteen. It would not be the only time Angelina was scarred in this way.

When Angelina was eighteen, she was hired to play her first adult film role. The vehicle, a sci-fi thriller called *Cyborg 2: The Glass Shadow*, was presented as a sequel, but it bore little relation to the original *Cyborg* film, released in 1989, which starred Jean-Claude Van Damme. The first *Cyborg* told a tale of evil gangs in a postapocalyptic world and was skewered by the critics. The second installment didn't fare much better.

In *Cyborg 2*, it's 2074 and androgynous cyborgs, which have replaced humans at all levels of society, are running amok. A ruthless (aren't they all?) corporation called Pinwheel has developed an explosive agent called Glass Shadow that can be injected into cyborgs. These androids may be used to achieve murderous ends. As the film begins we see Pinwheel executives watching a film of a beautiful (aren't they all?) female android having sex with her unsuspecting victim. Just as the cyborg reaches orgasm, she explodes, niftily blowing up her target and giving a whole new meaning to the term *in flagrante delicto*. Thanks to Glass Shadow, the powers that be at Pinwheel hold the combustible key to ruling the world—or at least to destroying their chief competitor.

Pinwheel's cyborg assassin of choice is Cash Reese—played by none other than Angelina Jolie—and she is unaware of the deadly fluid coursing through her nonveins. But once the wise and benevolent Mercy (Jack Palance) clues her in, Cash turns to human Colton Hicks (Elias Koteas), a martial arts instructor, for help. Together they struggle to evade a Pinwheel henchman as they make their way to a free zone where Glass Shadow is ineffective. Of course, they manage to pull it off and live happily ever after.

Cyborg 2, with all its firey explosions, entailed a lot of dangerous stunts, and it's fortunate that none of the stuntpeople who worked on the picture were seriously hurt. Movie special effects were becoming more and more spectacular in order to satisfy an increasingly sophisticated audience. The greater the effects, the greater the risk—inevitably, things would go wrong. The most horrific example of a stunt gone awry had occurred in 1982 during the filming of an episode of *The Twilight Zone*. Actor Vic Morrow and two children were killed when a helicopter crashed during the segment, which was directed by John Landis. In 1992, the year *Cyborg 2* was filmed, there was a rash of film accidents, mostly burns. Among the productions involved were *Toys*, *Private Wars*, and *Cyborg 2*. Industry and state officials were scrutinizing the situation, and they identified independent film companies as the primary culprits. California Deputy Fire Marshall Manny Chavez, whose job was to certify special effects crews and serve as an industry liaison, told Jeff Wilson of *Newsday*, "A smaller budget company has less to work with than a major studio. If they are making a movie involving special effects and stunts, corners may be cut." And California Film Commission director Patti Stolkin Archuletta agreed. "With smaller budgets, they are trying to do more spectacular stunts and explosions. But safety is one thing we can't compromise."

While appearing in B-grade action flicks may have been a hazardous way for a young actress to learn the ropes, Jolie didn't have to worry about special effects in her next film. For that matter, she didn't even have to worry much about bad reviews, because after it was screened at a film festival *Without Evidence* never secured a general release. The pseudo-documentary was a kind of extended *America's Most Wanted* episode, a cinematic attempt to uncover new information about the murder of Michael Francke, the director of the Oregon Department of Corrections who was stabbed to death outside the department's headquarters in Salem, Oregon, on January 17, 1989, when he was just forty-two. Written by Gill Dennis and *Oregonian* columnist Phil Stanford, the film puts forward the theory that a political conspiracy was behind the crime and that an innocent man may have been imprisoned for it.

At the time of the murder, it was widely rumored that Francke was about to expose corruption in the prison system. Speculation grew when Francke's family confirmed that he had told them he was about to go public with details concerning criminal activity within the agency he headed. But nothing seemed to come of this conspiracy theory, and the authorities finally arrested Frank Gable, a convicted drug dealer. In June 1991, Gable was convicted of stabbing Francke in the heart when Francke discovered him trying to break into his car. Gable, now serving a life sentence without possibility of parole, has always maintained his innocence, claiming that he knew who the real killer was and that this man had died several years earlier. In a curious twist, two of Gable's most loyal supporters were ultimately Francke's mother and his two brothers; recently, a judge has heard motions from Gable requesting DNA testing through which he hopes to prove his innocence.

The critics had scorned *Cyborg 2*, *Without Evidence* had practically vanished without a trace, and Jolie was in need of a better offer. She wanted a role that could advance her career, and she hoped that the part of Kate in director Iain Softley's *Hackers* would be it. Released in 1995, the film was one of the first to tap into the growing global fascination with the relatively new phenomenon known as the Internet. Softley had directed 1994's *Backbeat*, a story about the Beatles' early years, and it had met with critical success. He hoped to follow suit with *Hackers*, the tale of a group of high school computer junkies who stumble upon evidence that a multimillion-dollar computer fraud operation is afoot. The king and queen of this gang of cyberpunks are new boy in town Dade (played by Jonny Lee Miller) and Jolie's Kate—or, as they're known online, Zero Cool and Acid Burn. Years earlier, when he was just a kid, Dade managed to hack into over a thousand Wall Street systems. He was caught and ordered to stay away from computers until he turned eighteen. Of course, he can't comply with this sentence, and one night he picks up on a computer virus of unprecedented proportions created by a villainous master hacker who calls himself The Plague and who works as a security consultant for a major oil corporation. The virus will wreak worldwide havoc within days unless The Plague is paid off. When he realizes he's been discovered, The Plague frames Dade. What follows is predictable, but it's presented in a slick and entertaining fashion; plenty of computer graphics are laid on to inject color and flash.

If the film's producers were hoping that the new generation of computer aficionados would make Jolie and Miller its cyber pinups then they were disappointed. Both of *Hackers'* young stars admitted to being computer illiterate. Angelina seemed particularly proud to announce the fact during interviews to promote the film. "I hate computers. I write with a pencil. I'm scared of them. And I'm scared of breaking them." Miller also confessed that he didn't own a computer. "I know they have their place," he said, "but I don't need one. I'm not someone who needs to talk to someone in Russia at 4 A.M. on the Internet or store lots of information."

What did appeal to the sensibilities of both Jolie and Miller was the notion that hackers, with their subversive aura, were defenders of democracy. Jolie and Miller also insisted that hackers were not the shadowy figures the movie portrayed some of them as being. "They are very social—much more social than most people realize," said Angelina. "You can call them nerds, but they are good nerds. So many people sit at their computers from nine to five because that's their job. These guys do it because they love it." And Miller noted, "I think it's good that these kids have learned the technology, because if they hadn't learned it, we'd all be under the huge thumb of large corporations. It's not about hackers trying to break into banks to steal money. It's about trying to find out what information is being kept from people."

According to Jolie, the film had distilled the essence of hacker culture. "I think *Hackers* is about testing barriers, testing opinions. It's not just testing the limits around masculine and feminine; it's about testing barriers [between] different races, different sexes; everything being not what it should be . . . It was not about, 'Guys don't do this.' It was fun for all of us to try that. I think that hacker culture is experimenting with anything they want to do or be, about having the freedom to play, and maybe that seems queer."

Before he started shooting *Hackers*, Softley gave Miller and Jolie a crash course on computers so they wouldn't have to fake it onscreen. Almost in spite of herself, Jolie became captivated with the miraculous technology. "Even though I'm not into computers, part of me had fun," she said. "It's neat to push one little button and have everything happen." Laughing, she added, "Or have everything disappear."

When they weren't honing their computer skills, the *Hackers* leads spent a considerable amount of time on rollerblades; inline skating was yet another talent of Dade's and Kate's that Miller and Jolie did not possess. "We had three weeks of learning how to type and rollerblade, hanging out with the cast, which was heaven," Jolie told *Empire* magazine. "And racing Jonny on rollerblades was a big part of our relationship. We read a lot about computers and met computer hackers. With a lot of lines, I didn't know what I was talking about, but it was fascinating."

Unfortunately, when *Hackers* was released most critics didn't share her fascination. Ryan Gilby of the *Independent* called the movie "loud" and "silly." *Entertainment Weekly*'s Glenn Kenny smirked, "Hollywood is never goofier than when it's trying to capitalize on a trend it has no clue about. The makers of this teens-in-cyberspace caper film flaunt what little research they've done . . . creating a laughably unconvincing milieu peopled with sexy kids who dress like extras from *Blade Runner* and seem capable of creating new computer languages while rollerblading through Manhattan's Washington Square Park."

In a case of cyber irony, MGM/UA, the studio that distributed the film, fell victim to some real-life hacking. Several days prior to the film's release, a group of hackers, who had gotten a sneak peek at the script and concluded that the movie didn't do them justice, hacked into the MGM/UA Web site. They added a billboard that proclaimed the movie to be "lame" and "cheesy"; they posted comments like, "What Kool-Aid was to Jonestown, *Hackers* is to every cyberpunk movie ever made"; they defaced photos of the actors; and they replaced some publicity stills with a snapshot of hackers drinking beer.

Realizing that the press coverage generated by the cyber vandalism had created far more publicity than they could have paid for, MGM/UA claimed to be delighted with the pranksters. A studio press release noted, "We don't approve of their trashing our Web site, but we are thoroughly impressed by their creativity and ingenuity." Of course, the question of how, exactly, the hackers had laid their hands on the script to begin with continued to perplex studio executives. Jeff Moss, a hacker conference organizer, shed some light on the issue. He told the media that hackers hired as consultants on the film had passed along copies of the screenplay to friends via the Internet. The general consensus, said Moss, was that the film depicted hackers as immature.

However, two of the film's characters made a positive impression on a few critics. Harper Barnes of the *St. Louis Post-Dispatch* noted, "Jonny Lee Miller and Angelina Jolie star as teenage hackers who joust with computers but deep down are drawn to each other. They make an attractive couple, and some of their scenes together transcend the generally unbelievable script." Miller and Jolie's onscreen duets did, in fact, strengthen the movie's weak premise, but that wasn't entirely attributable to their acting abilities. If the scenes involving Angelina and her leading man crackled, it was partly because the two were falling in love.

Miller seemed perfect for Jolie. He, too, came from a family of actors, and he shared her desire to steer clear of the parental shadow. And Jonny, like Angelina, was a free spirit, willing to push it to the edge. Although most people who saw—or, more precisely, heard—him in *Hackers* never guessed it, Jonathan Lee Miller was an Englishman. He grew up in the middle-class section of Kingston-upon-Thames. His great-great-grandfather was an Edwardian music hall performer and his grandfather was the actor Bernard Lee, best known to a generation of filmgoers as M in the first twelve Jones Bond flicks. Jonny idolized his grandfather, who had a reputation for being a bit of an eccentric himself.

Jonny's father, Alan Miller, was a stage actor who went on to work at the BBC, where he remained for twenty years. Jonny has fond memories of hanging out with his dad at work, watching from the wings as various television shows were being shot. From the time he was a very small child, Jonny wanted to be an actor himself, and at ten years old he landed his first job, in the miniseries *Mansfield Park*. "I had to grow my hair long for that part and I got the piss taken out of me at school," he told Kate Spicer of *Minx*. Later, he attended the boys-only Tiffin School. "I liked it," he continued, "even though I'm not in favor of single-sex schools. When I was at that school, girls didn't exist, which is not a healthy attitude. You get guys coming out of school scared witless."

Because he'd decided so early what he wanted to do with his life, Miller felt constrained at school, and, as a result, he was a mediocre student. At sixteen, he left Tiffin and got a job at the Hard Rock Cafe in London's Piccadilly district. He actually viewed this as a career move. "I wanted to hang around these crazy, different people, and besides, it was fantastic, hilarious fun," he remarked to Spicer. "We all got free hamburgers." The high-spirited Jonny got into a few minor scrapes with the police during this time, but his stubborn determination to be an actor kept pulling him back onto the straight and narrow.

Miller's next career move was to take a job as an usher at the Drury Lane Theater. Working nights, he could go to auditions by day, and he began to get the odd television role. Among the first was a part on the Granada television series *Families*. "My only thought was that I did not have to wear this stupid blue uniform anymore and kiss the feet of American tourists," Jonny later maintained. "The reality, of course, is that you never stop looking over your shoulder wondering if the work is suddenly going to dry up."

It never did. Miller appeared in *Rough Justice, Meat, Speaking in Tongues, Bad Company, Goodbye Cruel World,* and *Prime Suspect 3*. He also won roles in stage plays, such as *Democracy, Beautiful Thing, The Neighbour, Entertaining Mr. Sloane,* and *Our Town*. At one point Miller was offered a contract to appear in the long-running, incredibly popular British soap *Eastenders*, but he turned it down. He reasoned that by going down that road he'd miss his chance to fulfill his true ambition, which was to be a film actor like his grandfather. In 1994, that chance finally arrived: he was cast as Dade in *Hackers*, and he traveled to Hollywood for the first time.

Although Miller didn't exactly describe his reaction to Jolie as love at first sight, he did tell a *Just 17* interviewer, "Well, she's a very striking woman and pretty hard to resist." The upside of romances that bloom on movie sets is that as long as the cameras are rolling the love-struck couple can spend their long working days basking in each other's company, cozily sequestered from real life. The downside is that when the movie wraps it's hard to transplant the romance into the everyday world. There's also the problem of maintaining the new relationship long distance—most actor couples find themselves shuttled off to new, and separate, film locations in short order. "We had a tumultuous affair 'cause we were living on opposite sides of the world," Miller admitted to *Just 17*. "But true love is something that just creeps up on you."

In March 1996, Jolie was twenty and Miller was twenty-two. They'd been carrying on their long-distance affair for about a year. Then, on an impulse, they decided to get married. It all came about so suddenly that Jonny didn't even get to meet his father-in-law, who was away filming *Mission Impossible* with Tom Cruise, until a couple of weeks after the wedding. "Being nuts about her had something to do with it," said Miller, attempting to explain what the rush was about. "But I also had to think it was a great opportunity to explore other worlds and to move and work in Los Angeles with a purpose. Otherwise I might have been asking 'What if?' for the rest of my life." Besides, as he said to Jane Ganahl of the *San Francisco Examiner*, "I couldn't let her get away."

Jonny and Angelina tried to keep their nuptials—held at Los Angeles City Hall with only two witnesses present—simple and quiet, but the pair clearly had trouble being low-key and inconspicuous. He was arrayed from head to toe in black leather, while she felt inspired to wear black rubber pants and a shirt on which she had painted her beloved's name in her own blood. Initially, the newlyweds made no public announcement of their status, but while in Europe promoting *Hackers* Angelina spilled the beans during an interview, commenting, "I always fall in love while I'm working on a film. It's such an intense thing. And I've always been at my most impulsive when Englishmen are around. They get to me. And, no, we didn't have a big white wedding.

Angelina with her first husband, Jonny Lee Miller

We had a small black wedding." At the same time, insisted Jolie, she viewed marriage as a romantic and noble institution. "There is no bigger deal than signing a piece of paper that commits you to someone forever."

Soon Jolie was displaying to one and all what would become her most notorious trait—her penchant for making wild, uncensored declarations that often left her interviewers unsure as to whether she was serious or playing a practical joke. In time, however, it would become evident that Angelina wasn't playing manipulative games. The only way she knew how to communicate was by offering up raw, often uncomfortable, truths about herself. She reveled in describing her fetishes for knives and tattoos; she freely discussed her sexual interest in women; she alluded to her curiosity about sadomasochism. And Angelina was pleased to show off her collection of tattoos, all of which symbolized something important to her. The one adorning her rear end was based on tribal totems from Borneo, the one on her arm stood for bravery, and the one on her shoulder was Death. She did get her symbols mixed up at one point, however. "I dropped my pants in a tattoo parlor in Amsterdam," Angelina told *People*. "I woke up in a waterbed with this funky-looking dragon with a blue tongue on my hip. I realized I made a mistake, so a few months later I got a cross to cover it. When my pants hang low, it looks like I'm wearing a dagger!" Like his bride, Miller was a tattoo fancier, as well—the snake on the inside of his wrist seemed incongruous, given his angelic teen-idol looks.

While *Hackers* didn't turn into a mainstream hit, enough teenagers saw it to make Miller the flavor of the month. He began popping up in teen magazines and on fan Web sites, but he didn't let it get to him. "It's flattering," he told Ganahl, "but it's not my agenda. Making really good movies is." First and foremost, Miller needed to see himself as an actor, because, "to believe otherwise would be vanity. I think most of that image is made up in magazines, anyway."

Prior to the European release of *Hackers*, Miller's star had risen considerably in Britain due to his riveting performance in *Trainspotting*, a film that would become an art-house hit in America later that year. Based on the novel by Irvine Welsh and directed by Danny Boyle, *Trainspotting* is an unflinching, though frequently funny, look at the lives of five Scottish heroin addicts. Exuberant, original, designed to shock, *Trainspotting* can be compared to *Drug Store Cowboy* in that when it first came out it offended conservative filmgoers with its depiction of drug addicts enjoying themselves. Both movies attempted to come to terms with reality rather than teach a simplistic moral lesson; both demonstrated that the life of the substance abuser may be hell on one level, but it's not devoid of pleasure, or humor, or fun.

Trainspotting's protagonists enjoy their drugs, but they pay a steep price. They confront AIDS and incontinence. They sink to unimaginable lows—the film's most infamous scene shows an addict diving head first into a filthy toilet to retrieve some dropped opium suppositories. There's no glamorizing of drug use here.

Miller's character, Sick Boy, is obsessed with Sean Connery and fancies himself something of a womanizer. The young actor was thrilled to be a part of this project, telling Ganahl, "It could have been irresponsible with the subject matter, but instead it shows the very bad with the very good." At that point, he was also wondering how such a movie would be received in the United States. "I mean, it's not like a Bond film, which all kinds of people will want to see. I think people will go, though, because they're curious. And you have to see it to decide if you love it or hate it! But I think they're going to love it." Many did love it, praising its bravery and its balanced vision, yet *Trainspotting* failed to become a mainstream hit in the United States. In the end, its chances for commercial success weren't sabotaged by its difficult subject matter. The problem was that the American ear could barely decipher its heavily accented, heavily idiomatic, rapid-fire dialogue.

Miller, however, didn't seem to mind. He was content to be anonymous in Los Angeles. He could tool around unnoticed and not be obliged to justify his whims to a watchful media. Imagine, for example, the outcry from PETA (People for the Ethical Treatment of Animals) had a tabloid reporter gotten wind of the fact that Miller and Jolie fed their pet albino corn snake (which slept at the foot of their bed) freshly killed mice. At home in England, of course, Miller was more closely scrutinized. Asked about his pet's dietary regimen by Christa D'Souza of the *Daily Telegraph*, he teased, "I won't tell you how I [killed the mice], because I'll have all sorts of people leaving bombs on my doorstep. But I will say I am very, very quick."

In retrospect, it seems inevitable that Jolie and Miller's marriage would be shortlived. Their relationship was intense, and passionate, and it finally consumed itself. In the first year they were together, though, their sexual electricity was obvious. Shortly after they were married, Jolie decided that she wanted some portraits of herself and her new husband, so she arranged a photo shoot with photographer Jeff Dunas. Speaking to Kate Spicer of *Minx*, Dunas said that Angelina had set up the shoot, "for the pleasure of it. You know when someone like Angelina wants to make pictures, they're wonderful results. As I remember, Angelina brought a lot of energy to the shoot. They were the exciting young couple. Wonderful subjects." Exciting, yes, but not conventionally romantic. Noted Miller, "We're not fans of heart-shaped things, not big smoochers."

Beyond their youth, their unsustainably intense sexual attraction, and their twin careers, there was a further obstacle to an enduring relationship that the couple just couldn't overcome: Jonny's homesickness. "One of the reasons we broke up was that I got fed up with Hollywood," Miller later said in an interview posted on the Internet. "I enjoyed it at first but I realized that Britain is the place to be, both for work and personal commitment. I know this sounds mad, but I was missing little things like *The Nine O'Clock News*, red buses, country smells, the sound of our rock music, and *Match of the Day*. Angie wanted to move to New York instead. I didn't want to experience a whole new town again, so I came back here and moved into a flat in London. But there are no regrets and no bitterness. Marriage was something that didn't work out, and I had to make the decision sooner or later. I decided to make it sooner." Miller's defection was also prompted by his sense that his career would suffer if he stayed in Hollywood. "No place on earth gets bored faster with new faces. You just have to remember all the failures—if you can remember their names."

For months after Miller's return to England, he and Jolie shrugged off questions about the state of their relationship. Then, nineteen months after their wedding, they made it official. In 1998, Angelina told Louis Hobson in the *Calgary Sun*, "Jonny and I are still crazy about each other, but we have the sense of needing to move on in different directions." Even so, she seemed reluctant to let go. "Jonny and I are divorced but we're still great friends," she revealed to Hobson in a 1999 interview. "We've literally held each other's hand through this whole ordeal. There's just never been a lack of love between us. I really enjoy talking on the phone and missing him. We love each other but we realize we can't do this marriage thing together at this time."

Jolie picked up this refrain again while talking to Deanna Kizis of *Harper's Bazaar*. "I didn't want to divorce him, but I had to, you know?" Being married to Jonny, she continued, not only helped her to be "a better woman," but it also taught her that she needed to be a little more trusting. "I am so self-sufficient that I don't know how to let a man be a man, or how to commit to buying a house together." Occasionally, Jolie expressed her regrets even more forcefully. "Divorcing Jonny was probably the dumbest thing I've ever done, but I don't dwell on it," she told Christa D'Souza. "Fortunately, he lives over here [in England] while I'm in New York. But we're still very close. I was so lucky to have met the most amazing man, who I wanted to marry. It comes down to timing. I think he's the greatest husband a girl could ask for. I'll always love him; we were simply too young."

Angelina's time with Jonny was a crash course in life—both personally and professionally—yet she wouldn't fully appreciate that until she'd gained the perspective of distance. Regarding her experience on *Hackers*, she recently told Christine James of *Box Office* that "it taught me a good lesson. I was just starting out, and I think a lot of young actors take themselves so seriously that unless we're crying and screaming, we don't think we're acting. There's something to just being present and being in the moment and having a good time."

THREE

CLIMBING SLOW

Those who make a living appearing on the silver screen often complain that film casting directors can't, or won't, see past an actor's last role—either that, or those in charge of casting are hung up on physical type, refusing actors the opportunity to portray a diverse range of characters. The obvious result of this blinkered approach—some would call it "lazy casting"—is that big-screen actors are quickly typecast. It's therefore not surprising that Angelina Jolie's next role was a *Hackers*-esque disenfranchised teen. The film was *Foxfire*, an adaptation of Joyce Carol Oates's novel *Foxfire: Confessions of a Girl Gang*.

The story unfolds in the 1950s and is set in a blue-collar upstate New York town. Five high school girls unite to form a gang, called Foxfire. Their aim is to display their pride and power for all to see; they also want to wreak vengeance against a culture that denigrates and destroys its young women. A press release promoting the book announces: "Here, then, are the Foxfire chronicles—the secret history of a sisterhood of blood, a haven from a world of lechers and oppressors, marked by a liberating fury that burns too hot to last. It is the story of Maddy Monkey, who writes it . . . of Goldie, whose womanly body masks a fierce, explosive temper . . . of Lana, with her Marilyn Monroe hair and packs of Chesterfields . . . of timid Rita, whose humiliation leads to the first act of Foxfire revenge. Above all, it is the story of Legs

Sadovsky, with her lean, on-the-edge, icy beauty, whose nerve, muscle, hate, and hurt maker her the spark of Foxfire, its guiding spirit, its burning core . . ."

Oates's novel, the press release continues, is "At once brutal and lyrical . . . charged with outlaw energy and lit by intense emotion. The story moves over the years from the first eruption of adolescent anger at sexual abuse to a shared life financed by luring predatory men into traps baited with sex. But then the gang's very success leads to disaster—as Foxfire makes a last tragic stand against a society intent on swallowing it up. Yet amid scenes of violence, sexual abuse, exploitation, and vengeance lies this novel's greatest power: the exquisite, astonishing rendering of the bonds that link the girls of Foxfire together—especially between Maddy, the teller of the tale, and Legs, whose quintessential strength and bedrock bravery make her one of the most vivid and vital heroines in modern fiction."

In the preface to the first edition, published by Dutton in 1993, Oates explains that "*Foxfire: Confessions of a Girl Gang* is very much a *girls'* story, and, as such, defines itself in sometimes playful but more often uneasy opposition to a male- and adult-dominated world. We sense that this opposition is not so easily maintained as the gang-girls imagine it might be. We sense that neither sex can live without the other; that the dream of a Foxfire Homestead, a Utopian sisterhood in the midst of a heterogeneous working-class world, is doomed. We sense that Legs Sadovsky, for all her intelligence, cunning, and idealism, is finally too reckless—too blinded by her own 'American-ness' to succeed . . . almost without being conscious of the transition . . . the Foxfire girls pass from childlike innocence to precocious criminality; at first victimized by adults . . . they become calculated victimizers themselves."

The premise is a strong one, and from it Oates constructed a compelling novel, but, as so often happens when a book of such narrative scope is adapted to a screenplay, a whole lot got lost in the translation. A key aspect of the book is that it was set on the East Coast in the 1950s, a time when racial, social, cultural, and gender discrimination in America was far more entrenched than it is today. The filmmakers, however, chose to set the tale in 1990s Portland, Oregon. Though the story's context was radically altered, its central premise remained the same: a group of high school girls form an alliance to combat a sexually abusive male teacher; the group dynamic is indelibly changed by the appearance of a mysterious new girl, Legs Sadovsky (whom director Annette Haywood-Carter describes as "James Dean").

The movie opens with a sadistic biology teacher (played by John Diehl) tormenting one of his female students, Rita, because she won't dissect her frog. He gives her a detention, and all the kids know he uses detention periods to sexually molest girls. So when Rita shows up for her after-school punishment she's not alone. With her are Maddy, Violet (one of the teacher's past victims), Goldie (who has a drug problem), and the enigmatic Legs. Spurred on by Legs, the girls leave the man battered and bloody. Suspended for their actions, the girls move into an abandoned house together and begin their descent into criminality. Think an adolescent *Thelma and Louise* without the wit or the depth.

Jolie, cast in the role of Legs Sadovsky, worried that *Foxfire* would get slammed for what might be perceived as its anti-male aura. Had the screenplay been more faithful to the novel, her fears might have been well grounded, but instead the film stumbled into forgettable melodrama, unworthy of controversy. Its one saving grace was that it contained solid performances by Jolie, Hedy Buress as Maddy, and Jenny Shimizu as Goldie.

A year earlier, Buress had been preparing to graduate from Milliken University, a small liberal arts college in Decatur, Illinois. "I was a stage actress," she explained to Susan King of the *Los Angeles Times*. "I was studying direction and acting. I had a band. That was my true passion. I was into rock climbing. I was doing a lot of things. In fact, I was backing away from theater more and more." Until, that is, she got a call from a Chicago-based casting director who had previously hired her to work on a CD-ROM game project. The casting director asked Buress if she'd audition for the role of Maddy. *Foxfire*'s Annette Haywood-Carter told King, "We had done the usual casting calls in L.A. and New York looking for Maddy. I was looking for a quality that was really fresh. Everybody I saw was wrong. I was looking for someone who everyone could relate to, particularly kids outside of the big cities." Within a week, Buress was flying to Los Angeles for a screen test. Two days after that she was hired, and shooting began the following week. Buress says she related to the *Foxfire* script because, "These girls were sort of taking their life with both hands and saying, 'You know what? I am going to start questioning life, I am going to question authority and I am going to question sexuality.' It's really being more aware of your choices."

Jenny Shimizu's choices have taken her down a strange path. Prior to being discovered in 1993 while hopping off her motorcycle in front of L.A.'s Club Fuck, she was a garage mechanic. Soon, her striking looks and her androgynous quality made her the first Asian American supermodel. Shimizu also became one of the few openly lesbian fashion queens, once remarking, "I've already been with every fine girl there is in the world . . . I've even French kissed Christy Turlington." Calvin Klein chose Shimizu for his hugely successful CK1 campaign; she's appeared in glossy magazine ads around the world; she was selected to become Tokyo's Shiseido model; and she is a hot runway model. "They like me because I don't care," Shimizu told *Curve* magazine, but then quickly added, "I don't take modeling for granted, either. I know I've been extremely lucky. I've had it so good."

Although she eventually wants to open her own car-repair shop, these days Shimizu is content to ride the show biz wave as far as it will carry her. *Foxfire* was her first film. "I absolutely loved this project because it felt so right," she explained to *Curve*. "You know when you find something and it just feels right? I know that acting is what I want to do . . . and there are so many strong girls in the film. It's about bonding. There's a lot of sexual tension, but no sex." Interestingly, Shimizu says that despite the fact that she's openly gay, she has never dated lesbians. "All the women I've gone out with are straight."

Enter Angelina Jolie. It was inevitable that she would bond with Jenny Shimizu, if for no other reason than they shared a passion for tattoos. "I love getting tattoos because they remind me of really happy times," Shimizu said to *Curve*. "All of the ones I have now I got at a really good time in my life." When *Foxfire* was made, Shimizu boasted five tattoos, including one of a woman straddling a wrench. Where the Snap-on logo should go the words "Strap-on" were inscribed.

Jolie reminisced to *Girlfriend*'s Diane Anderson, "I probably would have married Jenny Shimizu if I hadn't married my husband. I fell in love with her the first second I saw her. Actually, I saw her when she was being cast in *Foxfire*, and I thought she had just read for my part. I thought I was going to lose the job. I said to myself, 'Oh, my God, that's Legs.' She's great. We had a lot of fun." It could be that Jolie assumed Shimizu was reading for the part of Legs due to the ambiguous sexual energy both the actress and the character exuded. Jolie confessed, "I felt like Legs was a woman whose sexuality was always in question. I honestly could never see her in bed with somebody."

Legs's undetermined sexuality was, for Jolie, one of *Foxfire's* strengths. She was adamant that the film was "about friendship and bonding. I don't think the other girls came to any conclusions either. Legs was this woman who was very experienced in the world and if she had seduced Maddy it wouldn't have been right. Maddy had to figure it out herself. It wasn't my role to come in and turn them all gay. If they opened up and questioned themselves down the road—which you could imagine—that's what my role was, to open them up. It was not about us all fucking each other. I also felt like if Legs had been with anyone it would have been Goldie [Shimizu]. In the real world, she would have taken her as a girlfriend because they were most alike. In the movie, Maddy was her opposite, very innocent, and that's probably why they were interested in each other."

Jolie told Gary Dretzka of the *Chicago Tribune* that she saw Legs "as being androgynous, but sexual in a very animal sort of way: free . . . fascinating, intriguing, and touchy. The connection isn't directly about sex. I could see her being around it or watching it, but she is very much by herself. When a group of women or guys get together or mix, and they're together a lot of time, there's a curiosity—especially at that age. You're coming into your own and figuring out what people around you are like."

All the while, Jolie was doing her own "figuring out"; she discovered that she was not only attracted to women in the abstract, but in the flesh, as well. When it was all over, she acknowledged that she'd had an affair with Jenny Shimizu. Drew Mackenzie and Ivor Davis of Australia's *Women's Day* quoted Jolie as saying, "I'm quite free with my sexuality. I have a sinister sexual side, but there's also a side to me that's soft." It's curious that Jolie was implying her relationships with men brought out her dark side, while her liaison with a woman elicited a certain softness.

What surprised most people about the Jolie-Shimizu romance was not the lesbian aspect of it but the fact that it occurred not long after Jolie married Miller. "I think he's okay with it," Jolie said to Anderson. "He came to the set of *Foxfire*. He was around when I was figuring things out about myself . . . When I realized that somebody like Jenny could be a deep love for me, he realized it, and he took it very seriously. If anything, he didn't treat it just like some sexy thing."

Foxfire was released in 1996. Unfortunately, what audiences saw on the screen didn't begin to match the drama of the entanglements that had gone on behind the scenes. Wrote critic James Berardinelli, "there's no doubt about the lesbian leanings in *Foxfire*. The film never crosses the line from the unspoken to the acted-upon, but there are enough longing looks and pregnant pauses to make the reality of the situation apparent to even the most oblivious viewer. However, the issue of lesbianism is never confronted head-on, so we aren't given the opportunity to judge whether its inclusion would have made *Foxfire* a better motion picture." Although *Foxfire* had failed to engage Berardinelli, he did praise Jolie's contribution. "Angelina Jolie's Legs is a rebel with a cause . . . [Her] combination of sensuality and toughness makes for a beguiling portrayal."

Reviewer Martin Wong also gave *Foxfire*'s young stars a nod before panning the flick outright: "winning performances by Hedy Buress and Angelina Jolie and Jenny Shimizu's big-screen debut can't save *Foxfire* from spinning into self-parody. From its opening scenes to its melodramatic climax, Annette Haywood-Carter's directorial debut savages the sensibilities of the Joyce Carol Oates book from which it was adapted . . . *Foxfire* is less *Rebel Without a Cause* than *The Babysitters Club* gone bad." *Roughcut*'s Gary Susman gave *Foxfire* a thumbs-down, as well, accusing it of straining the audience's credulity. "The girls hide out in one of those beautiful, abandoned mansions that exist only in movies and enjoy a brief idyll of feminine solidarity (though it seems less brief during an endless sequence in which they tattoo their own breasts, proving that women's Iron Joan rituals can be as idiotic as men's)."

In the end, maintained Beth Pinsker of the *Dallas Morning News*, the film fails in a fundamental way. "Things fall apart when Legs gets sent to a juvenile detention center, leading to the inevitable point: Legs hasn't taught them to think for themselves; she's taught them only

to listen to her. The girls remain, as ever, loyal followers who respond to the strongest influence of the moment. They seem destined to end up as beaten wives. And that, above all, makes the film practically a criminal act against Ms. Oates's powerful fiction."

Both *Hackers* and *Foxfire* had evoked edgy, conflict-ridden worlds; both had tackled serious, timely issues in a mainstream entertainment format. And both had bombed. Jolie was ready to try her hand at something completely different, so she signed on to do a romantic comedy. *Love Is All There Is* was written and directed by the husband-and-wife team of Joe Bologna and Renee Taylor, who also starred in the film. Taylor's career had actually begun in the 1950s, but in 1996, when *Love Is All There Is* was released, she was best known for her recurring role on the television sitcom *The Nanny*. Taylor played Fran Drescher's mother on the show, and she received an Emmy nomination for that role the same year the movie came out. "It's nice to be discovered when you're sixty," Taylor told Anthony Scaduto of *Newsday*.

According to Taylor, *Love Is All There Is* tells the story of "a mother letting go of her son. My son married his childhood sweetheart when he was twenty-two and very early on I had to come to grips with letting go of him. The movie came out of that, with the idea of two warring families trying to stop the romance." Bologna and Taylor borrowed the framework of *Romeo and Juliet*, setting their take on the timeless tale in the Bronx of today; the warring families are rival catering clans the Cappamezzas and the Malacicis; and the star-crossed teenaged lovers are called Rosario and Gina. The two teens, played by Nathaniel Marston and Angelina Jolie, happen to be starring in a one-night community playhouse production of (naturally) *Romeo and Juliet*, and they fall head-over-heels in love. When they kiss in the last act of the play they hold the clinch far longer than the scene requires and have to be pried apart, to the horror of both sets of parents. When the young lovers sneak off and get married, the trauma becomes operatic in tone.

The film tries to get comic mileage from the fact that the clashing in-laws have completely different lifestyles, yet their reasons for keeping their love-struck progeny apart just aren't credible. The Malacicis are determined to ship Gina off to Paris to study ballet as preparation for marrying well, while the Cappamezzas don't want Rosario distracted from learning the family business. All of this prompted *Newsday*'s Jack

Mathews to grumble, "There isn't an understated moment or performance in the film, and much of the humor dissolves into annoying shrillness."

Reviews of *Love Is All there Is* were uniformly bad. The *New Jersey Star Ledger*'s Paula S. Bernstein wrote, "It's never a good sign when a film's main characters discuss the film's title. In fact, though it's never been proven, there seems to be a direct relationship between the number of times the title is mentioned in a film and how disappointing the movie-going experience turns out to be." In a *Box Office* review, Kim Williamson summed up the movie's most basic problem by noting, "Unwisely, Bologna and Taylor keep the focus of attention on the disputing adults . . . and away from the romantic couple. Lots of lame humor and uncomic contention ensue as the acting corps make sure never to let slip a chance to overplay their parts, making their turns as big and bangly as the bad jewelry and neo-seventies attire the women and men sport here."

Even if it appeared that more people worked on the movie than actually paid to see it, at least one person was delighted with the radiant Gina/Juliet. "I had the honor of doing script revisions for the film," said Erik Shapiro in a 1999 letter to *Entertainment Weekly*, "and was immediately taken aback by [Angelina Jolie's] talent after watching the audition tape of this young actress. It has been a pleasure watching her climb to stardom." In 1996, when *Love Is All There Is* was released, that "climb to stardom" seemed frustratingly slow. Any hopes Jolie may have had that venturing into the romantic-comedy genre would get her career in gear were dashed.

Her next project was to be an obscure effort called *Mojave Moon*. The plot-light script opens by introducing an L.A. car salesman named Al (Danny Aiello), who soon encounters a beautiful young woman named Ellie (Jolie) in a cafe. She flirtatiously asks him to drive her to her mother's Mojave Desert trailer-park home. He's so lonely that he agrees, but instead of falling for Ellie, he finds himself infatuated with her mom, Julie (Anne Archer). Over the course of the movie, Al butts heads with Ellie's jealous boyfriend, finds a dead body in the trunk of his car, and gets caught in the crossfire during a shoot-out between a gas station attendant and some would-be robbers. In short, everyone just gets a little crazy under the Mojave moon. Alrighty, then.

In just under two years Angelina had appeared in four films. Not one came close to a box office hit, but Jolie was wise enough to know that she was lucky to have steady work. She worked at maintaining a balanced professional attitude that proved to be a challenge because while most of the critics who singled her out in the reviews praised her acting, several took her to task. She told Gary Dretzka of the *Chicago Tribune* that she thought it dangerous to read too much into either extreme. "If you have enough people sitting around telling you you're wonderful, then you start believing you're fabulous. Then someone tells you, 'You stink,' and you believe that, too." It was hard not to listen to those voices, but Jolie knew that she had to do her best to ignore them and just get on with it.

FOUR

GOING FOR GOLD

There was a time when film actors studiously avoided working in television. In the first few decades of the small screen's existence, the only movie actors who appeared in America's living rooms were the ones who couldn't make it onto the big screen anymore. Prime time T.V. became a repository for cinematic has-beens, who were given cheesy guest spots on shows like *The Love Boat* and *Fantasy Island*. With the advent of cable television, all that changed. The made-for-T.V. movie, as broadcast on such channels as HBO and Showtime, was elevated to a new art form and the stigma associated with television acting began to evaporate. These days, the likes of Oscar winners Tom Hanks and Helen Hunt move effortlessly between the two mediums, enhancing their careers in the process.

Angelina Jolie's first role in a big-ticket television production was in the CBS miniseries *True Women*, based on the 1994 book by Janice Woods Windle, which follows a group of women over five decades spanning the Texas Revolution and the Civil War. Windle's characters were based on Texas's "founding mothers"—the Lone Star women who built homes on the frontier, bore children, and faced up to daily threats and obstacles posed by the Comanches, the Ku Klux Klan, and the soldiers from the North. In their spare time they participated in the suffragette movement.

Windle's inspiration was serendipitous. When her son Wayne announced his engagement, she wanted to present him and her future daughter-in-law with a special wedding gift, so she decided to collect family recipes and make a book of them. Calling on her mom, who just happens to be an historian, for help, Windle found herself in possession of an old scrapbook of handwritten recipes that her mother had stashed away. Among the recipes were stories about the family's history, and Windle included these in the wedding gift. When her children expressed their skepticism about the authenticity of the larger-than-life tales that Windle had framed as family history, Windle began to do some research. "I soon discovered that key women in my family tree were closely involved in the settling of the Texas territory," she says. Ten years later, *True Women* was published.

The book traces the lives of the Woods, King, and Lawshe families of Seguin, Texas—the hardships they endured, their personal acquaintance with the likes of Sam Houston and Santa Anna. While researching her novel, Windle read thousands of documents and interviews, but in the end she chose to focus primarily on three women who helped to settle the central Texas towns of San Marcos and Seguin: her maternal great-great-grandmother, Euphemia Texas Ashby King; her paternal great-grandmother, Georgia Lawshe Woods; and her great-great-aunt, Sarah McClure. As a young girl in 1836, Euphemia saw firsthand the aftermath of the Battle of the Alamo, which led to a mass female flight from Santa Anna's army. Years later she returned to Seguin where she married one of the infamous Rowdy King Boys, established a horse-breeding farm, and began the kind of family dynasty that would do Joan Collins proud. She survived Indian raids, panther attacks, and the political maneuvering that occurred as Texas first became a republic, then a state, then a member of the Confederacy, and finally a state again. As all of this was happening, Georgia Lawshe, the pampered daughter of a plantation owner, was forced to relocate with her physician husband to San Marcos. There the practical and pragmatic Georgia quickly established a thriving cotton plantation that managed to survive the Civil War. At one point, Georgia discovered that she was part Indian, and it changed her life.

Though *True Women* is technically a novel, Windle insists that everything, from the names of the characters to the places where the action occurs, is "absolutely accurate. My mother is a perfectionist historian. There are only three characters in the book who have fictionalized names, and they were real people. We just didn't have their complete names."

The CBS miniseries starred Dana Delany as McClure, Annabeth Gish as Euphemia, and Angelina Jolie as Georgia. Tina Majorino played the young Euphemia. Tony-winning producer Craig Anderson worked for a surprisingly long time to bring the novel to the small screen. On two occasions, he traveled to Austin to begin preproduction on *True Women* only to have the project canceled due to disputes over the projected costs. Finally, in the fall of 1996, Anderson struck a deal with Hallmark Entertainment, and the project was a definite go.

The miniseries was shot over seven weeks on location around Bastrop, Austin, San Antonio, Dripping Springs, and McDade. "Craig is one gutsy guy," Janice Woods Windle told Jane Sumner of the *Dallas Morning News*. "The book and the film both had to overcome hurdles of, 'Too Texas, too women, too many characters, too expensive.' I really do hand it to Craig because, from the very beginning, he said, 'Sooner or later, I'll get this to the screen.'" Anderson was determined to succeed in that endeavor because he'd already invested so much time and effort. He maintains that he spent over three years developing the script—and then he carried on right through the shooting. "The way that I make movies, I don't ever finish the writing process. I like to shape the movie as I make it. A lot of producers shape the movie in the editing room. I stand behind the camera at least ninety-five percent of the time."

To direct the miniseries, Anderson hired a woman. Female directors are still a relatively rare breed. "I always thought a woman should direct this," the producer told Sumner during an on-set interview for the *Dallas Morning News*. Explaining why he had chosen Karen Arthur, who had won an Emmy for directing the T.V. drama *Cagney and Lacey*, Anderson remarked, "She's getting values that a man wouldn't. I think a man's approach to this would be much more visceral with regard to action. He would probably look at all those sequences and do it like a John Wayne movie." Anderson, Arthur remembers, called her shortly after he had acquired the television rights to *True Women*. "He gave me the book to read and, of course, I fell madly in love with it." Making the project even more enticing for Arthur was the fact that Anderson recruited Arthur's husband, Tom Neuwirth, to be the director of photography.

Like many of the women who are directing film and television these days, Arthur started out as a performer. She worked as a dancer in New York City before relocating to Los Angeles, where she began directing theater. In 1974, she was selected to participate in the American Film Institute's first Directing Workshop for Women. It was a great honor, but it didn't mean that Arthur's battle for acceptance was over. "When I got my Directors Guild of America card," Arthur said to Sumner, "there hadn't been a woman director since Ida Lupino in the forties. There had been independent women like Shirley Clarke and others making experimental films and documentaries, but in terms of Hollywood, there just wasn't anybody." Surveying the professional landscape, Arthur decided that her best options were in television rather than the perilous world of feature filmmaking. In film, the competition was fierce and there was little margin for error if you were a woman (as Arthur commented to Sumner, "a man will have a chance to fail fifteen times and then succeed").

By the time she was offered the job of directing Anderson's miniseries, Arthur was a seasoned television director, well prepared to take on the task of bringing Windle's epic to life for CBS viewers. But Delany, Gish, and Jolie, the series' three leads, needed to do a little advance work. The trio of actresses spent a considerable amount of time visiting shooting locations, and they journeyed to Seguin to meet with thirty-eight of their characters' descendants. "I told them," Windle recalled to Sumner, "'You'll be able to see the story in their faces.'" Afterwards, the actors agreed. "That was great when I got to meet Sarah's great-granddaughter," said Delany. "She was just how you'd picture her. She was elegant, very sharp and walked with a cane. What's amazing to me is this is just one family's story. Probably every family in Texas has a story to tell. Hopefully, [*True Women*] will get them talking about it." Cast members were also taken on an excursion to Sarah's Great House at Peach Creek, an 1838 plantation house that sits on a flood plain. According to Windle, this was where Sam Houston warned area inhabitants that Santa Anna's forces were advancing, prompting five thousand women and children to head for the Louisiana border in a bid to escape the Mexican army.

True Women depicts a pregnant Sarah—accompanied by her young son, Johnny, and her sister, Euphemia—leading the terrified refugees across five raging rivers to safety. Windle had very much wanted to use the actual locations for events such as these in the miniseries, but the costs involved proved prohibitive. "If I ever get as much money as Stephen King," Windle later told Sumner, "I'd buy up the [town of Seguin's] doughnut shop, the beauty shop, and the Jack in the Box and turn the land into a park honoring all pioneer families."

In 1996, Windle finally got to see the story of her heroic ancestors on national television. *True Women* was one of the network's major projects that year, and so it was scheduled to air during the all-important May sweeps period. Leading up to the initial broadcast, the nerves of those involved were understandably a little frayed. Anderson sounded a touch defensive when he noted to Sumner, "They don't make these movies anymore. To be given the opportunity to do this, I really feel privileged. We all feel that way. All that true-crime crap and women-in-jeopardy and who-raped-whom psychological sickness that Americans have to watch all the time absolutely drives me up the wall."

For the most part, critics and viewers responded positively, even if some seemed cynical about the miniseries' orientation. Dusty Saunders of the *Denver Rocky Mountain News* wrote, "CBS bills *True Women* as 'an epic saga . . . a sweeping tale of love, war, and the American spirit.' Translation: *True Women* is specifically geared for female viewers during a sweeps month so far dominated by male-appealing shows dealing with Mafia violence and alien invasions . . . It's a frontier story that mixes petticoats with buckskin."

Steve Parks of *Newsday* crankily noted, "*True Women*, while described by its author as ninety-five percent true, suffers from the standard miniseries compulsion to turn real-life heroines into legends. Dana Delany struggles mightily to mold her character, Sarah Ashby McClure, into a flesh-and-blood woman. And though she largely succeeds—as does Annabeth Gish as her younger sister, Euphemia— the two are surrounded by impossibly caricatured men and women. Director Karen Arthur doesn't seem to know whether to make *True*

Women a *Roots*-like family saga or the made-for-T.V. women's movie of the week."

Yet others found the series' portrayal of pioneer women as heroines both refreshing and long overdue. "Movies and T.V. have traditionally taken the 'man's world' approach to frontier life (the white man's world, to be exact)," observed Chris Vognar of the *Dallas Morning News*. "The miniseries *True Women* takes great delight in debunking this myth . . . The dying perception that women played only a minor or subsidiary role in carving out Texas and the rest of the country has slowly been exposed as ludicrous." Most critics focused on Delany's contribution to the project, however, and Jolie was effectively upstaged.

In her next undertaking, which also happened to be for television, Jolie would again be part of a large ensemble cast. But this time her performance would be singled out, and she would suddenly find herself the subject of some real industry buzz, perhaps the single most important prerequisite for stardom. The project that would lead industry types to view Jolie with a new appreciation was the Turner network's riveting biopic *George Wallace*.

George Corley Wallace was born on August 25, 1919, in Clio, Alabama. He, his three siblings, and his parents lived in a four-room "shotgun" house, and like so many other southern families during the Depression they had to struggle to survive. There's little doubt that George's political leanings were shaped by the crushing poverty he experienced and by the boulder-sized chip on his father's shoulder due to the sorry state of the South's economy. George Wallace Senior would often tell his son that Southerners couldn't be elected to national office because Northerners considered them second-class citizens.

The charismatic George Junior set out to break through this barrier, and he rose swiftly through the political ranks. When he ran for governor for the first time, in 1957, Wallace did so on a liberal platform, and he enjoyed the support of the NAACP, the ACLU, and the state's Jewish population. But when he publicly opposed the Ku Klux Klan he lost the election. The executive producer of the biopic, Mark Carliner, notes: "Wallace wanted constant validation from the masses, and that's what drove him to power. He decided to wrap himself in the race issue to get elected." It was at this early point in his long career that George Wallace became racial segregation's infamous champion.

In the sixties the South embraced an apartheid-like social structure, and Wallace's popularity surged. "He sensed discontentment among the people and he intuited that the entire country was waiting to be 'Southernized,'" says Marshall Frady, on whose book the T.V. movie was based. "Wallace spoke in code to the issue of racial unease; he condemned the controlling powers in Washington that told citizens who to hire and where to send children to school, which was his code for racial antagonism. He alerted America's political management to a submerged continent of discontent that he himself helped activate."

Even those who weren't alive in the sixties are probably familiar with the more significant images of the decade: photos and news footage of the assassinations of the Kennedy brothers and Martin Luther King, the war in Vietnam, antiwar protests, race riots, and Governor George Wallace of Alabama defiantly blocking the entrance to the University of Alabama to keep out the school's first black students. His rise to power and fall from grace made Wallace one of the most controversial political figures of his time, and his name continues to provoke strong reactions among those old enough to have seen him in action. "Wallace is the Faust of our generation, a tragic hero who sold his soul," says the biopic's director, John Frankenheimer. "He was a fiercely intense and intelligent man in his time. He knew what he wanted, and the fact that he chose wrong is what this picture is about. This film either will or will not speak for itself, and people can offer criticism after they see it. But whether the audience is for or against George Wallace, I guarantee it will be emotionally moved."

There was a time in America when it seemed frighteningly possible that Wallace had the backing and the momentum to be elected president. But on May 15, 1972, while campaigning for the presidential nomination, he was shot five times by Arthur Bremer, a self-described assassin who had also stalked Richard Nixon and George McGovern. Miraculously, Wallace survived the attack, but his spinal cord was severely damaged. He was confined to a wheelchair and suffered constant pain. Despite his politics of division, Wallace had forged personal ties with some of his staunchest opponents, and among those who visited him during his recuperation were Ted Kennedy, Ethel Kennedy (the widow of Robert), African American congresswoman Shirley Chisholm, Richard Nixon, Hubert Humphrey, and George

McGovern. Even Elvis Presley, a longtime Wallace admirer, called and offered to avenge his friend's shooting; fortunately, nobody encouraged Elvis, who was by then battling his own chemically induced demons.

The assassination attempt triggered a drastic change in Wallace. "After he was shot, Wallace entered into a misery of spirit," says Frady. "He was oppressed by the deaths of Jack Kennedy, Robert Kennedy, and Martin Luther King, and wondered why he alone was the one who lived. When King's father visited him, Wallace apologized with tears in his eyes for being the one who survived. And from his wheelchair, Wallace begged forgiveness from the black congregation at King's former Montgomery church." Frady also told Bob Ivry of the *Record*, "I don't know if he mellowed as much as dimmed; his fierce edge had simply dulled. The ironic thing, of course, is that if he were never shot, this spiritual transformation, this remorse, probably never would have happened. There's still some question as to the authenticity of his contrition. But my feeling is one doesn't quarrel with reforms of the heart, no matter what the foxhole is."

Although he would never completely regain his political power base, Wallace did make a remarkable comeback. He learned to live with his handicap and worked to repair the social damage his policies had caused. He went on to serve two more terms as governor of Alabama, and a substantial portion of the state's black voters voted for him. He campaigned for the Democratic presidential nomination in 1976, and when he conceded defeat in the primaries he threw his support behind a fellow Southerner, the unabashedly liberal Jimmy Carter. At around this time he made a public confession, admitting that he had shifted his position to get elected governor. In an interview with John Kennedy Junior for *George* magazine, Wallace conceded, "Anyone who was running on a platform of integration back then would have been defeated in Alabama. I'm quite sure I would have been defeated if I had supported it." Wallace had come to realize that by opposing integration he had forever ruined any chance he may have had to be president.

Wallace's story is a layered and intriguing one, but what, specifically, induced Carliner and Frankenheimer to turn it into a film? "This story is an epic human tragedy," says Carliner. "It deals with three significant contemporary themes of American society: race and racism; the

fundamental danger of democracy; and forgiveness and redemption."
To Frankenheimer, the third theme was the crucial one. "If he were
just a bigot, we wouldn't have made this movie. This story is about
forgiveness and change. Prior to reading this script, I thought Wallace
deserved to suffer. I had no idea that he asked for forgiveness from the
blacks and became a born-again Christian. But Wallace is still responsible for a racial uproar that resulted in the deaths of four little girls in
Birmingham. Just because a man asks for forgiveness doesn't mean it
will be granted. Personally, I find it in my heart to forgive George
Wallace, but we're not advocating forgiveness. We're leaving that door
open; the audience can make its own decision."

Stage and screen actor Gary Sinise, who played George Wallace in
the film, had this to say: "Wallace was a symbol of resistance to civil
rights, but he eventually reflected upon his life and realized his mis-
takes. He apologized for his faults and asked for forgiveness, and he
tried to replace a legacy that was extremely difficult to live down . . . At
the end of this movie, people will know that he apologized for his
actions—but even more will know that he stood in the [University of
Alabama] door."

The filmmakers based their script on the book *Wallace* by Marshall
Frady, who lived in Montgomery during 1966 and 1967, when Wallace
was laying the foundation for his national podium. The former
Newsweek, Life, and ABC Television journalist was so close to the
Wallace team that he was asked to become Wallace's press secretary.
"He had a fascinating power to engage and enchant with spryness and
wit," says Frady. "Wallace came alive when he was swimming among
the multitudes, and he possessed a folk genius for connecting with
the people and sensing what the particular mood or humor was at that
time." Frankenheimer agrees: "Like Franklin Roosevelt and Winston
Churchill, he had a unique ability to make people think he was speaking directly to each of them. An interpretation of Wallace as a one-
dimensional villain would be inaccurate, because there is a side of him
that was charming."

Wallace's personal relationships were complex and his life had
moments of high drama, so casting the biopic was a formidable exercise.
The actor who played Wallace would have to age twenty years onscreen
and make the film's subject believable and human through all the

At the *George Wallace* premiere with costar Gary Sinese

challenges and changes he experienced. So Frankenheimer offered the part to the talented Sinise, who was very happy to accept. "The script was so well written," says Sinise, "and John Frankenheimer is such a passionate and inspirational director, that I couldn't pass up this project." When it came to casting Wallace's two wives, Lurleen and Cornelia, the filmmakers turned to Mare Winningham and Angelina Jolie, respectively. Lurleen was Wallace's first wife, and she died of cancer. According to Winningham, she was "the dutiful politician's wife who sacrificed her health when she ran for governor [sponsored by her husband]. She would have done anything for her husband, and she ended up giving him her life." After Lurleen died, Wallace married Cornelia, the niece of his political mentor Big Jim Folsom. Jolie characterizes Cornelia as "a fiery Southern woman who matched Wallace's energy. She was attracted to his confidence and passion. I think she always loved him and would have stayed with him, but he eventually forced her out."

Frankenheimer, who calls Angelina "a director's dream," notes that Jolie brought out the bimbo-ish side of Cornelia, the opportunist, the vulnerability, the sorrow. You saw the loss." Speaking to *People* magazine, Frankenheimer raved, "The world is full of beautiful girls. But they're not Angelina Jolie. She's fun, honest, intelligent, gorgeous, and divinely talented. She brings a hell of a lot to the party."

These days most cable movies are shot on location in Canada, where production costs are significantly lower. The team that made *George Wallace* wanted to shoot some of the footage in Alabama, and the locations were arranged, but those plans had to be scrapped at the last minute; the film was ultimately shot in Los Angeles. "The current governor of [Alabama] made it clear that we were not welcome," explained Frankenheimer. "That negative climate and the economic benefits of staying in California led to our decision, and the fact that we stayed out of Alabama did not have any affect on this film." That "current governor," Fob James Junior, had made the following public announcement: "I wish the scoundrels who are producing this fanciful work of fiction would stay out of this state. They are not fit to trod on Alabama soil." Frankenheimer had little patience for this attitude and vigorously defended his project to *Variety*'s Army Archerd, "They want us to whitewash George Wallace. We're showing a part of Alabama history. It has our respect—but we're not a documentary, we're a drama. It's a drama based on real events. I think the people of Alabama will love this movie. It's important. Racism is still a strong issue in this country. That's why this picture is so important. There's a whole generation that doesn't even know about George Wallace—there are people working on this picture who don't even know George Wallace."

But despite their determination to base their drama on real events, the filmmakers did exercise their creative license in one instance; and thereby drew criticism from many quarters. They fabricated a composite character called Archie, a prison trustee employed by the governor as a domestic aide. It was done with the best of intentions, maintains Carliner: "Archie metaphorically reflects the black consciousness of the time. There were certain people in the black community who had an enormous seething resentment against Wallace, and Archie represents this climate."

Terry Kelleher of *People* gave *George Wallace* a B and expressed reservations about the character of Archie, played by former *Mod Squad* star Clarence Williams III. "Compared with the historical liberties taken by Oliver Stone in *JFK* and *Nixon*, the dramatic license in this miniseries may seem trivial. But writers Paul Monash and Marshall Frady invite criticism by inventing the character of Archie . . . Although Williams and Sinise have some strong scenes together, we grow suspicious of the way the quiet servant is used as a sounding board for the politician's evolving racial views. When a wheelchair-bound Wallace, two years after surviving an assassination attempt, finally makes a public renunciation of his past bigotry, Archie is conveniently on hand to provide validation and a form of absolution—in case the viewer needs some extra convincing." Kelleher did, however, approve of the film's depiction of Wallace's marriages, remarking, "As for the temperature of Wallace's private life, it soars after his first wife, Lurleen (Mare Winningham), dies and the younger, sexier Cornelia (Angelina Jolie) becomes Alabama's first lady."

While some critics seemed underwhelmed by Jolie's performance—*Dallas Morning News* television critic Ed Bark cracked, "Ms. Jolie contributes a few semi-textured scenes . . . but probably would be better suited to a chicken-fried version of *Melrose Place*"—most included her in their praise for the cast as a whole. Wrote Virginia

Rohan of the *Record*, "The whole cast is top-notch . . . Angelina Jolie plays Cornelia, the sexy second wife, who stood by her husband when he was shot (but they divorced, messily, in 1978)." *Newsday*'s Liz Smith concurred. "The political and cultural sweep of the movie is riveting, but I was most impressed by the scenes of intimacy between Sinise, Winningham, and Jolie—emotional, intense, and magnificently performed."

Everyone who worked on the film was anxious to see how *George Wallace*, the movie, would be received by those who were portrayed in it. Frankenheimer met with Wallace himself prior to the release of the film; the former governor of Alabama was seventy-eight at that point, deaf and bedridden. "He could stop you just by looking at you," Frankenheimer told the *Record*'s Bob Ivry, "And even in that state, you could see the politician at work." Wallace's only comment to Frankenheimer about his film biography was, "I hope I live to see it."

In the end, members of the Wallace family, who had at first expressed animosity towards the project, were pleased with the epic four-hour life story. Wallace's son complimented Winningham's portrayal of his mother, Lurleen, and Cornelia Wallace was happy with Jolie's rendering, insisting that the young actress had played her scenes perfectly. Many Hollywood insiders agreed. Jolie would eventually receive an Emmy nomination for her depiction of Cornelia Wallace. She failed to win the coveted statuette, but she had little cause to regret it. Soon afterwards she bagged a Golden Globe for Best Supporting Actress in a Series, Miniseries, or Movie.

While the Emmy Awards and the Academy Awards are arguably the most hotly contested prizes in the television and film industries, respectively, the Golden Globes have a growing cachet. The winners are chosen by a handful of foreign journalists, and this, coupled with the fact that past winners include the likes of Pia Zadora, has tainted the Golden Globes to some extent. So has the popular notion that if you treat enough members of the foreign press to lunch you improve your chances of winning dramatically. But what has given the Golden Globes their current clout is their proximity to the Oscars, their unique combining of television and film awards, and the fact that they are televised. And, the truth is, the Hollywood community loves attending the Golden Globes because, unlike the more formal Oscars and

Emmys, they are one big party from start to finish. Guests are wined and dined (and wined some more) prior to the ceremony, and during it, and after it. They are seated at tables with their costars and friends instead of being ranged in auditorium seats. The mood is convivial, the liquor flows, and, as a result, the acceptance speeches are actually spontaneous and entertaining.

Angelina Jolie's coming-out party took place at the Hollywood Foreign Press Association's fifty-fifth annual Golden Globes presentation, held in the Grand Ballroom of Merv Griffin's Beverly Hilton Hotel. As the event got under way, stars of the big and small screens made their way to their lavishly laid round tables. Among those in attendance were Leonardo Di Caprio and Kate Winslet, stars of *Titanic* (which would go on to snatch up a truckload of Golden Globes and Oscars); Matt Damon, who had been nominated for both acting and writing in *Good Will Hunting*; and Helen Hunt, who had earned Best Actress nominations for her television series *Mad About You* and the film *As Good As It Gets*. These luminaries mingled with other high-profile nominees—Steven Spielberg, Jim Carrey, David Duchovny, Gillian Anderson, Jada Pinkett, and the casts of *ER* and *Friends*—as well as a fleet of notable presenters, such as Madonna, Goldie Hawn, and Mel Gibson. Angelina Jolie had also been asked to present an award that night, clearly a nod to her second-generation status.

She performed that task with aplomb, but on her next trip to the podium her heart was likely pounding a lot harder. She had been called to accept the Best Supporting Actress Award. Taking the trophy from presenters Brendan Fraser and Minnie Driver, Jolie looked genuinely astonished and a little flustered. After uttering a few general words of thanks, she gazed down at the statue and then scanned the audience. "Dad, where are you? I love you," she called before walking off. Jolie later remarked that she'd felt as if she was having an out-of-body experience. "I was totally in shock. Like I crashed a party and someone gave me the okay to stay."

It was quite an occasion. To place Angelina's experience in context, here are a few other high (or low) points of the evening. Michael J. Fox took the stage to present the Best Actress in a Drama Series award, and when he announced that *Chicago Hope*'s Christine Lahti was the winner nothing happened. Fox looked out at the audience expectantly, waiting for Lahti to jump up from her seat, but she was nowhere to be seen. This was because she had run off to the bathroom, not realizing that her award category was next. To fill up the time it took for frantic Golden Globe officials to track down Lahti, Robin Williams did a brief comic bit. When Lahti finally rushed onto the stage, looking harried and still wiping her hands, she gasped, "I was just flushing the toilet when someone said, 'You won!' I thought they were joking, and I was thinking, 'What a bad joke.'"

Later, *ER*'s Anthony Edwards, who picked up Best Actor in a Drama Series honors, quipped as he accepted his award, "I guess I could just pee right here."

Then there was Ving Rhames. Accepting his award for *Don King: Only in America* he was overcome by emotion. He professed that it was a great honor simply to be placed in the same category as his fellow nominees and unexpectedly called one of them, Jack Lemmon, to the stage. Looking wary, Lemmon joined Rhames, whereupon Rhames presented Lemmon with the award. An embarrassed Lemmon tried to make Rhames take it back, to no avail. All the exasperated show biz veteran could do was exclaim, "This boy is crazy."

And those guests who took the time to look through the Golden Globe's souvenir program that night would have noticed that tennis star Andre Agassi had taken out a full-page ad declaring his undying love for Brooke Shields. (The couple would marry a short time later.)

After the ceremony, the winners mingled with reporters and other guests. Jon Voight was beaming. The proud papa could be heard to announce, "Angelina has evidenced such mastery of acting. She has great desire to do good work . . . When we talk, I'm mostly just amazed that she knows as much as she does. It's really more a sharing of information, and I love hearing her unique approach to things. It's always wonderful when I speak with a real artist. As a father, of course, I'm especially delighted and moved."

When it was all over and done with Jolie confessed to Conan O'Brien and his late-night audience, "I got really drunk. My dad was with me and so in the beginning of the night he was really proud of me and then after I started downing tequila he was like, 'Oh, do you think that's a good idea?' And then he left." She also said in a press interview that she'd encountered Voight again at a post-awards party. "Suddenly, he became My Dad, saying, 'Are you sure you need another shot of tequila at 5 A.M.?' I'm, like, 'Dad, what are *you* doing here?' It was funny."

While such antics may well have enhanced Jolie's reputation for being wild and free, the fact that she'd won a Golden Globe put Hollywood on notice. The message was that the time had come to take Angelina Jolie seriously: she was much more than Jon Voight's daughter or another pretty face; she was wild and free and extremely talented.

FIVE

UNSCATHED

Few would deny that layered, meaty film roles are a rare commodity—especially those suited to young actors and (particularly) actresses in the early phase of their careers. And the very nature of the film business makes changing this state of affairs a difficult process. For one thing, it costs the major studios an enormous amount of money to make a feature, so producers hedge their bets. One way they do this is to manufacture products that will sell internationally—specifically action-adventure movies. Another is to sign a very bankable—and very expensive—star such as Tom Cruise or Harrison Ford to the project. The stakes are high due to the staggering overhead figures involved, but the potential for huge profits is there as well. This game is for serious players only. Everybody else just watches from the sidelines.

Small features do get made, however. Success stories like *Good Will Hunting* and *Shakespeare in Love* were made for a fraction of what it would cost a studio to produce an action-adventure flick, and they offer hope that studios will continue to bankroll the types of projects that provide complex and interesting roles for actors and actresses alike. A lead role in a relatively low-budget feature makes an excellent stepping stone to the big time for the young star-in-the-making—like Angelina Jolie. Also, such roles are a wise choice for the television star looking to access the big screen—like David Duchovny. After all, if a small film bombs the residual effects are far less severe than they are if a highly publicized big-budget feature dies a gruesome death at the box office.

In 1997, there were few television actors more popular than *X-Files* star Duchovny, who was inclined to present himself as the antistar, one who disdained the trappings of television celebrity but had no problem using his small-screen rep as a means to become a film star. Duchovny didn't even develop an interest in acting until he was well into his twenties. Prior to that, he was deeply involved in an academic career, working on a doctorate in English at Yale University; his dissertation was titled "Magic and Technology in Contemporary American Fiction and Poetry." He was also a talented athlete but while an undergraduate at Princeton he discovered that he wasn't good enough to make the university's basketball or baseball teams. In 1982, Duchovny graduated summa cum laude from Princeton and then moved on to Yale.

While still a Yalie, Duchovny was lured to New York City, but his dream wasn't to make his mark on the Great White Way. He just wanted to earn some good money tending bar. A friend of his happened to be an actor, and he suggested to Duchovny that he might do better auditioning for commercials. The only acting experience Duchovny had was a small role in a Yale playwriting student's production, but he still took his friend's advice. "He brought me to an audition and I got a couple of callbacks," Duchovny told Carla Hall of the *Los Angeles Times*. In the meantime, he found an agent who was willing to take him on if he agreed to enroll in some acting classes.

Before long, Duchovny's academic pursuits were simmering on the back burner and acting had become a full-time undertaking. Duchovny was twenty-eight at that point, well entrenched in the academic life, and the transition wasn't a smooth one. "There was a period there," he told Hall, "when I decided to become an actor when I was probably doing the worst work I'll ever do and having the worst success. I'm glad it worked out, because it was certainly a stupid thing to do."

Duchovny was given small roles in several films, including *The Rapture* and *Kalifornia*. He was also the narrator of the erotic Showtime cable movie (later a series) *Red Shoe Diaries*. One of Duchovny's more memorable early roles was the transvestite FBI agent in David Lynch's television series *Twin Peaks*. Although the show had rocked television conventions and enthralled audiences for a while, its appeal was flagging by the time Duchovny joined the cast. Coming out of *Twin Peaks*, he had lower expectations of his next high-profile project, the lead in a new, supernatural, sci-fi-themed series for the Fox network. But *The X-Files* was a huge popular and critical hit. Duchovny and his costar, Gillian Anderson, were catapulted to T.V. stardom. Fame just didn't sit well with Duchovny, however. "I understand why people get a little nutty, but it's annoying too," he complained to Hall. "Some people grab you. You're walking around in your little bubble and all of a sudden there's somebody grabbing your shoulder and you're, like, 'What?' Yeah, I'll say, 'Don't touch me.' And then it's like, 'Ooh, what a jerk.' There is no way to win in any situation."

Soon, however, Duchovny was looking on this erosion of his privacy as the price exacted by success. He realized that he had to maintain his focus on the job at hand. "Whatever money or power that I get from being able to choose what I want to do because of doing this show, that's incidental," he explained to Hall. "The most important thing for me is that I'm ready to do my best work now because of this show, because I had to go to work every day, 250 days out of the year. And act. If I had gone from doing one or two movies a year, I would have never gotten that self-training. That's been the greatest gift of the series for me."

Although plans had already been finalized for Anderson and Duchovny to star in an *X-Files* feature film, *Playing God* came along first. This film was to be Duchovny's first opportunity to capitalize on his small-screen success as Fox Mulder, his *X-Files* persona. Almost as soon as he signed on, however, problems arose. Two weeks prior to the start of production, the film's original distributor, Columbia Pictures, backed out citing "creative differences" (the all-purpose excuse) with the film's production company. Then Touchstone stepped in to re-place Columbia, and everyone involved in the project tried to settle down to work. Still, Duchovny admitted when speaking to Rebecca Ascher-Walsh of *Entertainment Weekly*, "It's disturbing because you go, 'Have I signed on to do a project that sucks?'" Angelina Jolie may well have been asking herself the same question, because she had committed to *Playing God*, too.

In the film, Duchovny plays Dr. Eugene Sands, a surgeon who loses his license. Sands, it seems, was high on amphetamines while performing an operation, and his patient died. Lack of sleep has driven Sands to become addicted to speed, and when the picture opens he's a guilt-ridden junkie. One night, many months after being stripped of his medical license, Sands is buying drugs at a Los Angeles nightclub when a couple of hit men walk in. They pump several rounds into a man who is sitting at the bar near Sands. The shooting is so obviously gangland related that no one present wants to get involved. The victim collapses in a puddle of blood. Hesitating only briefly, Sands comes forward and clears the blood from the wounded man's lungs using a wire coat hanger and the tube from a soda dispenser. Once he knows that the man will survive, he rushes out of the club to avoid getting busted for practicing medicine illegally. But his heroic act has been noticed by an attractive woman named Claire, played by Angelina Jolie, who has secrets of her own.

As it turns out, the shooting victim works for a local crime boss named Raymond Blossom, played by Timothy Hutton, and Claire is Blossom's moll. A few of Blossom's henchmen kidnap Sands and take him to their leader but the mobster only wants to thank the doctor for saving his cohort's life. He gives Sands ten thousand in cash for his trouble. Suddenly Sands has a new and unwanted calling—Blossom coerces him into becoming the crime family's doctor. Sands tells himself that at least the money will pay for his drug habit, and he even manages to form an uneasy friendship with Blossom.

But, of course, things rapidly get more complicated. FBI agents contact Sands and compel him to act as their informant. And then Sands finds that he's attracted to Blossom's woman. To make matters even worse, Sands's conscience begins to trouble him as he saves the lives of a succession of criminal types by performing surgeries in hotel rooms with Blossom's men as his assistants. When Blossom extracts some information from a man Sands has treated and then shoots the man in the head, Sands is finally jolted out of his moral ambivalence. His spiritual epiphany comes when he realizes that the greatest narcotic he has ever experienced is the emotional high he gets from healing people. The stage is thus set for the film's rather predictable ending.

Duchovny, generally reluctant to give interviews, worked the television talk show circuit diligently in order to promote *Playing God*. It was hard work. He was clearly ruffled when his *Today* show interviewer asked him about the difficulties involved in transforming oneself from a television star into a film actor. "If Robert De Niro had started in *Charles in Charge* he still would have had the career he had," Duchovny retorted. "I think it's just fate." In several press interviews, Duchovny said that he was drawn to *Playing God* because he thought the character of the defrocked doctor was unique. "You've seen this character in movies when bad guys get hurt and can't go to the hospital so they go to the bad doctor. I'd never seen him as a focus of a movie, and I thought that was an interesting story to tell."

For Jolie, the film was a pleasant diversion, in part because it provided her with the most grown-up role she'd ever had. "That was very rock 'n' roll and fun and loud and say-what-you-want-to-say, dress wild and love wild—you know that fantasy," she told her dad in *Interview* magazine. "I really allowed myself to get into that world. Being the age I am, I sometimes feel like a punk kid walking onto certain sets, but I didn't this time. I felt very much a woman." Working on the film was also enjoyable for Jolie because the project was better funded than some of her previous ones had been. "On a lot of the independent films I've been on, it's been so difficult to pull things together," she told Gary Dretzka of the *Chicago Tribune*. "You're really rushed for time, and there's only one change of wardrobe. You have to be careful not to get a stain on it."

It helps, as well, when your boss is your biggest fan. *Playing God* coproducer Melanie Green remarked, "[Angelina's] very beautiful and everybody will be clamoring for her. She has the wisdom of an old soul . . . the grace and style of an older woman. You want to peel away the layers when you meet her." Still, Green admitted, Jolie wasn't what they'd been initially looking for: "In the beginning we thought Angelina was too young . . . we didn't know how old she was. Angelina was the last person we saw on the last day of auditions, and she was just awesome. The thing about Angelina is that you can't say she looks like anybody else . . . Audrey Hepburn, maybe."

Jolie's character was supposed to be the object of sexual desire for the characters of both Duchovny and Hutton, although the scenes in which they satisfied their lust didn't make the final cut. "I had sex scenes with both [David] and Tim," announced Angelina. "They cut both of my sex scenes. With David we were basking in sunlight, and with Tim we were fucking hard in the back of a car. I think they felt like they couldn't have one without the other so they cut them both." Later Jolie told *Movieline*'s Michael Angeli, "My gut feeling was they cut the Tim sex scene because they decided they wanted to make a clean, action-type film. I thought it should've been about two people who change each other, like *Pretty Woman*. People love the idea of changing each other, don't they?" Jolie then added that in her love scene with Duchovny, "My character had just gotten shot and I couldn't move because I had a purple breast. And there were, like, a thousand candles. They always do that—put all these candles in the big sex scenes. I have never had sex like that in real life."

In those erotic scenes that moviegoers never got to see the chemistry must have been right—Jolie was very fond of her two leading men. In fact, press reports linked her romantically with Timothy Hutton, although representatives for each of them squelched the rumor by insisting that the two were just good friends. Of Duchovny, who had wed actress Téa Leoni a few months earlier, Angelina commented, "It was nice working with [him] . . . He was very sweet."

Try as the cast members might to promote *Playing God*, it was a tough sell. Duchovny valiantly pronounced it "a good movie," but apparently his heart wasn't in it. *Playing God* is "not the movie I wanted to make," he continued. "Like a lot of movies, you think something going in and you want to make a certain movie, but then it takes on a life of its own, something Frankensteinian." He also said that he had trouble with the film's conclusion. "In the end, my character's redeemed because it's a Hollywood movie," he told Ascher-Walsh. "I didn't want to redeem him, but there were other people involved."

Eugene Sands may have been redeemed Hollywood-style, but *Playing God* couldn't be saved. It opened on October 17, 1977, grossed a paltry $1.9 million, and hit bottom with a thud. Critics competed with each other to come up with colorful ways of condemning it. CNN online reviewer Paul Tatara noted, "Anybody who can convince Téa Leoni to marry him must have a personality, but if that's the case, Duchovny certainly manages to keep it under wraps during the hour-and-a-half it takes to wade through the movie . . . The man simply does not do a thing. He just stands there and watches everybody act. At one point, a woman whom he has the hots for takes a bullet in the chest,

Dancing with Peta Wilson at the 19th Cable Ace Awards

and Duchovny responds as if he's watching his ol' hound dog yawn. The only thing that makes the scene interesting is the fact that the actress, Angelina Jolie, sports magnificent lips that look like a couple of overstuffed Barbie Playhouse sofas."

While the *San Francisco Examiner*'s G. Allen Johnson actually liked Duchovny's performance, nothing else about the film captured his fancy. "*Playing God* is . . . one of those films where everyone's got a snappy reply loaded and ready, the personalities involved are a bottled series of quirks—not actual characters—who are subservient to an outlandish, over-sized plot that is in turn subservient to some hazy idea of *style*. Hutton—a long way from *The Falcon and the Snowman*—pushes the accelerator into self-parody. His British punk-rock get-up and ever-increasing hostility make it impossible for him to relate effectively with either Eugene or Claire . . . In *Playing God*, style is the false idol these filmmakers prostrate themselves before."

If Duchovny took the lion's share of the critical heat, then Jolie was practically ignored by many reviewers. "Duchovny, who also narrates the story, marches through the proceedings with the stony gaze of someone under anesthesia," noted Robert Denerstein of the *Rocky Mountain News*. "And Timothy Hutton, as the villain, goes as far into excess as possible, creating one of those impossibly *colorful* bad guys who could exist only in a movie. A low-profile supporting cast doesn't add much. Angelina Jolie stars as the sexy woman in the mix."

Still, a couple of established scribes seemed delighted with Jolie. Wrote Michael Medved of the *New York Post*, "Angelina Jolie . . . makes a knockout impression as Hutton's languid, leggy mistress; with her lavishly luxuriant lips, shiny, brittle (and broken) surface, she's nearly perfect as a wounded neo-noir heroine." And *Newsday*'s Jack Mathews mused that Jolie "gives her femme fatale Claire a world-weariness beyond her years, plus a hint of intelligence that contradicts her circumstances."

There was a lot of critical speculation as to whether Duchovny would survive this perilous transition from television star to film actor. Mathews had his doubts, remarking: "*Playing God* is Duchovny's film to rise or fall upon, and the elevator is definitely not going up." Yet somehow Angelina Jolie had costarred in a bomb and walked away unscathed. If anything, her stock had risen. No one was ridiculing her for making poor career choices—they were too preoccupied with the question of what this intriguing young star would choose to do next. Many were eager to know whether a professional pairing of Jolie and Voight was in the cards. For his part, Voight embraced the idea. "She's come along very quickly and I'd very much like to work with her," he told Susan King of the *Los Angeles Times*. "We're keeping our eye open for that possibility." During an *Empire* magazine interview Jolie concurred, then elaborated, "But it would depend on the situation. I know he loves to direct, but for anyone who has the possibility of their father directing them, the rebel that was in them when they were thirteen would just come out—the 'I'm not going to listen to you!' attitude."

Still, Jolie's most immediate concern was the overall quality of the roles that were then being offered to her. "I seem to be getting a lot of things pushed my way that are strong women, but the wrong type of strong women. It's like people see *Hackers* and they send me offers to play tough women with guns, the kind who wear no bra and a little tank top. I'd like to play strong women who are also very feminine." So when *Hell's Kitchen* cropped up and Jolie was invited to play the tough-yet-soft Gloria, she was pleased to accept.

Besides Jolie, *Hell's Kitchen* starred Rosanna Arquette (as Jolie's mother, of all things), William Forsythe, and Mekhi Phifer, who at the time was generating a lot of industry buzz. Entertainment reporters lapped up his life story. Phifer was born in Harlem and raised by his mom. When he was sixteen he decided that the only way to earn decent money was to sell drugs. However, his life of crime ended in less than a day. "I stepped out of myself," he recalled to Dan Jewel of *People*, "and I looked at myself on the corner, looking out for undercover cops and looking for rival drug dealers, and I was like, 'What am I doing here? My mom raised me better than this.'" Before long, Phifer had found a legal way to bring home the bacon: film acting. He made his screen debut in Spike Lee's 1995 drama *Clockers* and went on to appear in *Soul Food* and *I Still Know What You Did Last Summer*.

In *Hell's Kitchen* Phifer plays a young man named Johnny. As the story begins, Johnny participates in a botched robbery, which results in the death of one of his accomplices, Hayden. Hayden is the brother of

Johnny's girlfriend, Gloria, played by Jolie. Johnny is caught and sent to prison, where he learns to box. When he's released, five years later, he is determined to turn his life around by becoming a boxer, but he's shaken to discover that Gloria blames him for her brother's death and wants him taken out. Johnny is also thrown off-kilter when he learns that his mother has died and his own younger brother has vanished. Furthermore, training at the boxing gym is no picnic. Although an ex-boxer named Lou takes Johnny under his wing, Lou's former manager skulks on the fringes looking for fights to fix. Trouble just keeps brewing, and Johnny comes to realize that before he can move forward he must confront his past and clear his name.

Hell's Kitchen was released in 1998. Once again, the critics turned their thumbs down. And once again, Angelina Jolie emerged from the debacle unscathed. Ernest Hardy of the *New York Times* enthused, "With those impossibly sexy lips, stunning body and a screen-flooding presence, she drags all eyes onto her. More incredibly, though, she delivers as an actress once she's grabbed your attention. And she gives *Hell's Kitchen*—an interesting misfire of a film—a weight and center that it doesn't always deserve."

Critic Lawrence Van Gelder blamed writer/director/coproducer Tony Cinciripini for the movie's shortcomings. "Little about this film . . . is convincing." Cinciripini "has cribbed together a host of familiar characters, plotlines, and situations and tried to jumble them into something new. He doesn't really succeed, because while Rosanna Arquette as Gloria's junkie lounge-singing mom almost steals the movie, and Phifer and Jolie are two of the most gorgeous actors in Hollywood (always a joy to watch), none of them have anything to really bite into. Their characters are curiously flimsy, despite the grimy circumstances they go through."

Michael Atkinson of *Mr. Showbiz* agreed. "Cinciripini never . . . displays the basic knowledge of where to put a camera, or how to pace a scene, write believable dialogue, or direct actors to do anything more than drop their r's and exchange their th's for d's. Too big for this tripe by half, Angelina Jolie and Mehki Phifer clearly need new agents; Rosanna Arquette and William Forsythe need entirely different careers. This is the kind of dime-store, mean-streets indie we saw a lot of in the initial post-Tarantino gold rush, so Cinciripini's disasterpiece doesn't even feel like one of the worst movies of this year, but of 1993."

Up until this point, it almost seemed as if Jolie was biding her time, reining in her talent until she found the right project in which to unleash it. Finally, in 1998, the role she'd been waiting for landed in her lap.

SIX

TRAGIC SOULMATE

"I've always wanted to be really curvy. I need to exercise soon because my body looks like a twelve-year-old's when I don't. I'm starting to lose my butt, and my arms look pathetic." Speaking to a *People* interviewer after being selected for that magazine's "The Fifty Most Beautiful People in the World, 1998" feature, Angelina Jolie was typically chatty yet self-revealing. She worried that she was devolving from sexy woman to waif—but, in fact, her slender frame would help to qualify her for her next project, the controversial HBO film *Gia*. Based on a screenplay by Pulitzer Prize-winning playwright Michael Cristofer, the cable T.V. film would push the boundaries of small-screen drama and deposit Jolie at center stage.

The "Who else could have played that part?" game is a popular one in Hollywood, but it wasn't much fun when it came to *Gia*. If ever a role seemed created specifically for Angelina Jolie, *Gia* was it. One suspects that on some level the real Gia, who is now considered the first of the supermodels, and Angelina were soul mates. One essential difference between the two, however, is that Angelina learned to conquer her demons in a far less self-destructive way.

Gia Carangi was born on January 30, 1960 in Philadelphia, the daughter of a South Philly hoagie shop proprietor. When she was eleven, her mother walked out on the family, leaving Gia and her two brothers to be raised by their father. Although Gia and her mother, Kathleen, did reestablish their relationship a couple of years later, the sense of abandonment that had overwhelmed Gia at such a sensitive age would never leave her, and it would become her primary emotional motivating force. As a teenager, Gia began taking the occasional modeling job, including some work for Gimbels. One night, when she was seventeen, she was out dancing at a Philadelphia gay club called DCA when stylist and would-be photographer Maurice Tannenbaum approached her and asked if he could take some pictures of her. Gia agreed and at the shoot she met a woman who knew Wilhelmina Cooper, a former top fashion model who owned one of the world's most important modeling agencies. The woman took Gia to New York to meet Wilhelmina. Gia announced herself by carving her name with a switchblade into the agency receptionist's desk. Regardless, after spending just fifteen minutes with Gia, Wilhelmina offered her a contract. Gia returned to Philadelphia and mulled over the offer.

"I'd just gotten out of high school then," she recalled, speaking to *Philadelphia Magazine*'s Maury Levy. "And I was just cruisin' around. You know how Philly is when you're young and trying to have fun. So I had this choice. See, I smashed my car up and the insurance company was giving me two thousand dollars, right? So it was either take the money and buy a new car and stay in Philly and drive around and have a good time, or take the money and go to New York and try to do something with myself."

Gia's parents reacted differently to Wilhelmina's offer. Her mother supported the idea, spurred on, perhaps, by the fact that she herself had dreamed of being a model when she was younger. Her father had his doubts. "I never got the right vibes from him," said Gia. "Maybe he didn't like the idea that they wanted me to give up my last name." In the end, Gia signed the contract and moved to Manhattan. There, despite her exceptional self-confidence, she felt a bit intimidated. "I was scared of the city," she admitted, "because it seemed so huge compared to Philadelphia. And there was a lot of snow, and I had to take a lot of taxis, and I didn't know how to hail them, and I didn't know my way around, and it was really kind of freaky."

Gia's first modeling assignments were modest, but she quickly moved up in the pecking order after meeting photographer Arthur

Elgort at a job. He was so impressed with her that he introduced her to people at *Vogue* and *Cosmopolitan*. Among Gia's new acquaintances were top photographers Francesco Scavullo, Chris von Wangenheim (who specialized in pictures that captured the madness of the disco era), and Richard Avedon. Everyone began requesting Gia for their shoots. At that time, most first-rank models were the classic blonde, blue-eyed patrician types such as Christie Brinkley, Cheryl Tiegs, and Patti Hansen, but the dark-haired Gia offered the fashion world a fresh alternative. Suddenly she was gracing the covers of the big glossy magazines. By the time she landed her first major print ad, for Gianni Versace, she was earning $100,000 a year. She was eighteen years old. By 1980, after she had become top girl at Wilhelmina's, she would be earning five times as much.

Gia's dark coloring was part of her appeal, but she was also a desirable model because she was able to change her appearance with ease; she could look sophisticated, streetwise, or innocent—whatever the job required. Yet Gia's personal style was the antithesis of haute couture. she favored black leather motorcycle jackets and men's apparel from vintage clothing stores. Gia was unique and captivating and those who moved in fashion circles fully expected her to enjoy a long, successful career. She was flying high, and few could see that the seeds of her eventual self-destruction were being sown.

Not only was Gia one of New York's most sought-after faces, but she was also one of its most sought-after bodies. Hordes of men longed to seduce her, but they were destined to be disappointed. Although Gia did occasionally sleep with men, her true interest lay elsewhere. Long before sexual preference was an open topic of conversation, Gia was an unapologetic, sexually aggressive lesbian. She frequently made passes at other models, especially when they shared hotel rooms with her on location shoots. "She was always that way," explained Jolie, who had been granted access to Gia's journals. "When she was about thirteen, her mother found letters she had written to girls in school."

As a top model, Gia was welcome to patronize any nightclub she wanted, and before long she'd immersed herself in New York's glittery nightlife, which at that time centered on Studio 54. In that scene drugs abounded, and Gia was furnished with an endless supply of whatever she desired; at one point or another she desired them all—pills, coke,

booze. Ultimately, her mind-altering substance of choice would become heroin. The signs of her addiction—the canceled shoots, the
complaints about the bright lights, the chronic lateness—were there
for all to see, but most people chose to attribute them to the fashion-
model temperament. In late 1979 an incident occurred that in retrospect seems quite telling. Gia canceled two weeks of bookings,
claiming that she didn't like the way her hair had been cut. She holed
herself up in her apartment and refused to come out until her locks
had grown sufficiently.

At other times, Gia could appear entirely rational and in control of
her life. When Maury Levy asked her in 1980 if she worried about
growing old, Gia, then nineteen, laughed the question off. "Nah. I'm
gonna get out before that happens. Because I feel satisfied already from
modeling. I did it, you know what I mean? I made it." She later told
Cosmopolitan that when her modeling days were over she wanted to
find a new occupation. "I want a job where I can be out of the lime-
light, making things happen, possibly cinematography. Modeling is a
short gig—unless you want to be jumping out of washing machines
when you're thirty."

By 1982 Gia had been a major presence in the modeling world for
four years. The shift in her outlook that had occurred during this time
was captured in a quote from the book *Scavullo Women*. Although she
was only twenty-two, she claimed to feel as if she were "going on
eighty-four." In the legendary fashion photographer's book, Gia also
reminisced about her early days in New York. "It was fun. A lot of
models have a rough time, but things started happening pretty quickly
for me." She then admitted there was a steep price to pay for all that
fun. "When you're in demand, and people are saying, 'I want you, I
want you,' it isn't easy to say no. I don't like to disappoint people; I'm
basically a satisfier. So you find yourself working a lot—*a lot*! And if
you want to take a day off, because you need a day to rest or to get
yourself together and have your energy for the next day, it's hard. Models
are never supposed to be down or be tired or have a headache. They've
got to be *up* all the time!"

Before filming began on HBO's *Gia*, Jolie had to participate in
several days of fashion shoots that re-created some of Gia's most famous
assignments. "I hated just changing clothes and posing. I felt that if I

did that all the time, day in and day out, that I'd feel like a big piece of me was being ignored, and it would drive me mad." The vicarious experience also reaffirmed Jolie's personal rejection of the values modeling tends to promote. "When you're trying to put yourself together and decide the kind of woman you want to become, you look at different images of women. But my heroes were actors and musicians."

The fashion world's skewed values, those that Jolie so adamantly rejected, may or may not have played a part in Gia's descent into drug addiction. But whatever it was that made her drug dependent, Gia's plight was an open secret by 1982. Gia herself knew that her behavior would no longer be indulged or overlooked as it had once been, so in *Scavullo Women* she acknowledged that the rumors about her were true and tried to explain. "I think the reason someone gets into something like that is because for me, anyway, there were a lot of unanswered questions in my mind about work and about life. Money didn't interest me. I got to a point where I had all this money. I had everything I ever wanted and I said, 'What the hell is this all for?' I learned a lot from my experience, so I don't regret it. It was good for me, like a slap in the face. I'm an extremist, you know, I had to go all the way."

She had to be something of an extremist to maintain the kind of body that could sell a client's product or image. Gia was five feet eight inches tall, and in order to keep her weight at 120 pounds she ate mainly fruits and nuts and periodically subjected herself to juice fasts. Obviously conflicted about this, she denied worrying about her weight when she spoke to Levy. "Sometimes I even like to get pudgy," she insisted. "I think it's cute. I don't like to be real thin. Sometimes I see these other models, they take their clothes off and I think, 'God, give this girl some beef.' They're usually real bony, like chickens. They're always ordering health food. I hate it. I order a hamburger. I mean I get off on food, you know. I'd rather do food than any kind of drug."

As time went on, Gia struggled to sort out the good values from the bad, yet drugs gained a greater and greater hold over her. She fought to stay grounded—telling *Cosmopolitan*, "When I get out of work, I throw on a T-shirt, jeans, and my sneaks just to get back down to earth"—but staying grounded proved to be a losing battle. When Wilhelmina died of lung cancer in 1980 Gia never emotionally recovered from the loss. Whatever stability she had left began to dissolve. Former model Janice

Dickinson told Mimi Avins of the *Los Angeles Times* that she recalled Gia showing up "two hours late for a shoot. Then it took the makeup artist three hours to make her look decent. And then she passed out face down and ruined her makeup. Gia was always doing things like that. We were all just so naughty then."

As her drug use accelerated, Gia's behavior became not just erratic but also violent; on one occasion she discovered one of her female lovers with a man and hurled herself through a car windshield. Gia also had a fascination with knives, and she was known to have brandished them at people she felt had slighted her. Her arms and hands became covered with needle tracks and open sores. Scavullo, one of her first mentors, continued to hire her, hoping that the work would somehow turn her around. It didn't. Eventually Gia was reduced to selling jeans in a Pennsylvania shopping mall. Amazingly, she was finally able to kick her habit, but it was too late. Her body was already failing. In 1986, after being blackballed from the modeling profession, living in a welfare hotel, and getting mugged and raped, Gia was diagnosed with AIDS-related complex, which she'd contracted through intravenous drug use. She asked her mother to take her in and she refused. But when Gia died on November 18, 1986, Kathleen was by her side. Gia Curangi is now considered one of the first women in America to have died of AIDS-related complications.

In 1993, Stephen Fried published an engrossing biography of Gia entitled *Thing of Beauty: The Tragedy of Supermodel Gia*. Paramount had purchased the rights to it but then sat on the property for several years. An honest movie about Gia would have to contain depictions of lesbianism, drug use, and violence, and no major studio was at that point prepared to touch two of those three issues. Then, in February 1997, *Variety*'s Army Archerd reported that HBO had announced it was making its own two-hour movie about Gia, to be written and directed by Michael Cristofer (who had won both a Pulitzer and Tony for *The Shadow Box*). Marvin Worth would produce.

Worth acknowledged to the entertainment press that in light of the film's subject matter he was surprised that HBO was moving ahead with it, "but at the same time, the love scenes are really tender and not gratuitous." HBO Pictures president John Matoian explained that HBO had to branch into new territory and provide something that the major networks weren't offering. "There's no secret to the fact that we need to be distinctive. But what I love about *Gia* is that it's tackling an edgy subject matter that's also slightly more female skewing, which has not necessarily been the traditional NBO audience or movie."

Although Cristofer had never met Gia—in fact he'd never even heard of her before the project was pitched to him—there was a connection. As a successful Broadway playwright in the late seventies and early eighties he'd traveled in many of the same circles, went to many of the same clubs, and knew many of the same people as Gia had. "We're just getting far enough away from it that it appears different to us," Cristofer remarked to Mimi Avins. "Gia's time was my time. From 1977 to 1982 was my fifteen minutes of the glamorous life in New York. I had a play on Broadway and was getting a lot of attention. I was at Studio 54 and hanging out with the Warhol crowd. Because it was before the AIDS crisis, that time had a quality of exuberant freedom that we miss. A lot of us got away with a lot. And a lot of us didn't."

Cristofer prepared to write the HBO script by reading Gia's journals and interviewing people who had known her. His mental portrait of the young supermodel gained color and nuance. What intrigued him most was that "Across the board, everyone seemed to have a different view of her. And it lets us off the hook in saying this is *the* accurate portrait of her because it's based on our impression of what we could learn." Cristofer's primary objective was to avoid portraying Gia as a victim. "Everybody wants simple stories with obvious rights and wrongs," he said. "But people are inexplicable, and even a Shakespeare would have a difficult time with her."

While Cristofer's approach to Gia was a compassionate one, his attitude towards the modeling world was contemptuous. "I think the whole fashion industry is truly disgusting. And the current fascination with that world by the entertainment industry is more than disgusting. It's immoral. The notion that models are being treated like talent is, to me, one of the worst things going on today in Hollywood."

Another theme that Cristofer extracted from Gia's story and worked into his screenplay was loss of innocence—on the part of the individual and her society. "Despite all that was going on" in Gia's milieu, he mused, "there was an innocence to it all, because people weren't aware of how dangerous it all was. That's gone." Marvin Worth voiced a related sentiment while speaking to Alanna Nash of *Entertainment Weekly*. Both Hollywood and the modeling world, he maintained, are "hard on your maturity. Gia was a baby. I don't know too many actors or actresses who aren't babies. The problem is, models and actors live in fantasy worlds. To come through it is a victory."

Then Cristofer had to face the problem of writing a biopic of a person whose friends, relations, and associates are still living. Certain people, Cristofer said, objected to being included in the film, "So I went ahead and used composites of people or left people out who posed legal problems. Then I started getting letters from people saying, 'How could you leave me out?' So it was problematic." One person who didn't complain was Francesco Scavullo. Cristofer told Valerie Kuklenski of the *Los Angeles Daily News* that he thought Scavullo's relationship with Gia was "very kind." In the book *Scavullo: Photographs, 50 Years*, Scavullo wrote, "Photographing Gia was like shooting a movie. She moved continuously, not a single pose. There was a kindred spirit between us."

Without question, the movie would be made or broken over the casting of Gia. Surveying the Hollywood talent landscape, Cristofer and Worth were searching for someone who possessed not only Gia's physicality but also the acting skills to bring her mercurial character to life. More than two hundred actresses auditioned, including Angelina Jolie. But Jolie had her reservations about the part, later explaining that she'd thought it would "drive me a bit nuts to be that open. I didn't want to do it. I didn't want to go to that place. It was such a heavy story and dealt with so many issues. If done wrong, it could have been very bad and not said the right things, and it could have been very exploitative."

What convinced Cristofer to go with Jolie was a certain essence she shared with Gia. "Angelina is probably as adventurous a person as Gia in many ways, even if she didn't act on those impulses," Cristofer remarked with diplomatic understatement. "And she has the quality which I'm told Gia had—a pervasive innocence and vulnerability, which I thought was a quality desperately needed. In the hands of the wrong actress, I think Gia could be a person you didn't really want to be in the same room with."

Jolie, however, was still not sure that she wanted the role. "It was really tough," she admitted to Diane Anderson of *Girlfriends* magazine. "When I first got the script I avoided it. There was a lot of the story that I really identified with, so I didn't want to touch it. I just didn't want to deal with it. She had a lot of pain. Gia was emotionally and literally raped, but she had such a fire for life and . . . love for women. She had these incredibly crazy moments, and she was always attacking everything she wanted, just going for it."

The kinship Jolie felt with the doomed model may have been uncomfortable but it was also undeniable. "Just the part about figuring out who you are," continued Jolie. "Wanting the world to be so much and watching everyone else have so much less enthusiasm. People not understanding your craziness when you're all excited about something, but they want you to calm down. Not ever feeling completely full." In the end, of course, she rose to the challenge. "We went over the script for an afternoon and [Michael Cristofer] convinced me. I think everybody involved with this film was coming from a place that was very deep inside them. [Gia] was so human to us, and we all loved aspects of her and we all identified with certain things. It became very personal. Gia has enough similarities to me that I figured this would either be a purge of all my demons, or it was gonna really mess with me. I hate heroin because I've been fascinated by it. I'm not immune, but I won't do it now, at all, because luckily I've found something that replaces that high, which is my work. And, probably because I didn't want the part, because I was scared of where it would take me, the producers knew I was right for it."

Cristofer was entirely convinced. He knew that Jolie had both personal and professional reserves to draw on as she became Gia. "She's serious about acting in a very real-life sense," he commented. "It's a big part of her existence and her identity; it's not a show-off thing or a look-at-me thing with her, although there is always that element in acting. But I think she really does use it as a way to understand and know herself. She's a hunter, you know, a real adventurer."

Interestingly, Jolie's first introduction to Gia was a 1983 20/20 interview with her. Gia was obviously stoned, yet insisted she was sober. "I hated her," Angelina recalled. "She was acting her butt off. She had this very affected speech and seemed very vacant. I didn't believe a word she was saying and it was really hard to watch. Just really sad." By the

time she'd viewed a few more tapes, however, Jolie was softening. "She was talking and being herself, just this regular girl from Philly, and really out there and funny and bold and I fell in love with her. I think deep down that she was a good person who wanted to be loved. She had a great heart and a great sense of humor and just wanted more excitement."

Rounding out the cast of *Gia* were Faye Dunaway as Wilhelmina, Mercedes Ruehl as Gia's mother, Kathleen, and Elizabeth Mitchell as Gia's lover, Linda. Cristofer selected Mitchell over two other hundred other actresses after seeing her in Edward Albee's *Three Tall Women* on Broadway. Mitchell's career was launched in 1994 on the ABC soap *Loving*—an experience that was anything but warm and fuzzy. "I was a perfectionist," Mitchell admitted to *People* magazine. "I'd tell the writers, 'I can't say this!' So I got fired."

Some actors still worry that playing a gay character will negatively affect their careers, but not Mitchell. She maintained that she thoroughly enjoyed playing Jolie's on-screen lover. "We did this one love scene on the bed where we were laughing so hard we were shaking, the whole bed was shaking," she told Natasha Stoynoff of the *Toronto Sun*. "The director was yelling, 'Stop it! Stop it!' Angelina and I tried to think of sad things so we wouldn't laugh, but everything we thought of became absurd and funny, so it got worse and worse and worse." Then Mitchell added, "She's got such beautiful lips and they're all her own. She's all real. She's a work of nature. She hasn't put herself together at the plastic surgeon's office . . . My character is very much like me in real life—she's very straight-laced. Angelina is different. She's this force of nature. She is a firestorm."

Jolie was equally at ease with the love scenes, admitting to Elizabeth Snead of *USA Today* that, like Gia, she finds women sexually attractive. "People keep asking, 'What was it like to sleep with a woman?' It was fine, it was nice; she was beautiful. What's the problem?" Pursuing the topic with Amy Longsdorf in *Playboy*, Jolie said, "I really don't see anything physical as being that important. I mean, I don't see women, men or black, white. I don't see a handicapped person; I just see the person. I see the aura, the energy."

As Angelina delved more deeply into the character, her understanding of, and empathy with, Gia grew. "You think beauty and fame and money should make a person happy?" she asked. "I don't think so, if you don't have love and you don't have people to share it with. I think a lot of people have that feeling inside, that we don't think that people care about who we are inside or understand us." Jolie had quickly understood that the seminal event in Gia's life was her mother's desertion of her. "If I didn't have my mother, if she left when I was eleven, you know—God. I would have been looking for that my whole life, that kind of love and comfort." In the end, Jolie felt that Gia's drug use, her close relationship with Wilhelmina, and even to some extent her attraction to women, stemmed from her lifelong desire to fill the void that was created when her mother walked out the door.

Mercedes Ruehl, whose job it was to depict Kathleen, came to a similar understanding. Speaking to Alanna Nash in a *New York Times* interview, she said, "Drugs are a manifestation of the problem, but the real problem is the wound. In the screenplay, we have a mother with a narcissistic wound and a daughter who is narcissistically wounded herself, from a kind of heartbreaking neglect. They're both having to get through the day with massive tricks of denial. Certainly, in this screenplay, [Gia] experienced the beginning of the profound under-standing that can only come through suffering, in walking through a refining fire. She really had a quest to her soul. She just had no one to help her. In the end, she becomes someone who is impossible to easily judge, because she kept trying to hold on to something with meaning. My guess is that on a spiritual level, Gia achieved a great deal."

As the filming of *Gia* progressed, Jolie's emotionally draining adventure intensified. She embraced her character, but at the same time she guarded against being engulfed by her. She told Snead that Gia "had so much inside that no one knew, that quiet, private, intense and brilliant side—everyone just thought she was wild and pretty. She's the closest character to me that I've ever played. But in an odd way, playing Gia has made it possible for me not to ever become her. The difference is I have a job that isn't completely about my exterior. It's about my work, my mind and doing characters, speaking, and talking. I'm able to let it all out and she couldn't."

Some days the glamor of it all was elusive. Jolie told Conan O'Brien about filming the fashion-shoot scene in which Gia and Linda first connect. "I kinda take my clothes off and do the photo shoot behind the fence, which is what Gia did. And I tried to get this makeup artist [Linda] to also take her clothes off, and meet her at the fence, and it was her come-on. She was really wild. So, it was this big sexy day, and I was really waiting for it. So, I wanted to not eat too much and be really healthy for it and really sexy for it. So, earlier in the day I had a scene where I was supposed to be taking black beauties, and so I ate all these charcoal pills. And right before the love scene, I threw up— black—all over the place and then was forced to eat something. Then I was kinda bloated and upset and really nervous."

Despite this small catastrophe, Jolie's professionalism showed. Mercedes Ruehl told Laurie Sandell of *Biography* that throughout the difficult filming Angelina's "courtesy . . . was unfailing. She was always on time, always prepared for some heavy emotional stuff. No actor can do take after take like that without some serious technique in her background." By far the most trying scenes to film for everyone concerned were those in which Gia was at death's door. She'd lost all of her hair and Kaposi's sarcoma lesions covered her body. "I really looked like I was dying," Jolie said quietly. Angelina believed that Gia finally found peace at that point. "She got back to her sense of humor and she forgave people and she talked with the people she loved. She was seeing very clearly at the end of her life. There's something so beautiful about that—that she went through it all and did find herself in her last moment."

But Gia's biographer, Stephen Fried, disagreed. He told Mimi Avins, "People in the business are fooled by the camera into thinking that if you can take a pretty picture of someone, there must be something okay about her. Before Gia, it never occurred to them that you could be that amazing a model and that close to the edge of your life. She isn't a model who just had some problems. This girl did not go back to Oklahoma and live a different kind of life. She died. Everybody thinks the worst thing that could happen if you send your teenage daughter to New York to be a model is she wouldn't be successful. The worst thing that could happen is what happened to Gia."

What happened to Gia will remain a matter of interpretation, it seems. No matter how evenhanded and touching a biopic turns out to be, it is inevitable that some of the people who were close to its subject will be unhappy about it. In the case of *Gia*, the bone of contention was the apparent lack of input from some of Gia's intimates—such as Rob Fay, who befriended Gia in rehab; Kathleen; Gia's brother Joe; and her aunt, Nancy Adams. "I don't understand," Joe Carangi Junior said to Diana Marder of Knight Ridder, "how they make movies about people and where they get information without talking to people who knew her. When she was a model she was just used. And the movie is evidence that she's still being used."

The critics, though, thought the movie was evidence that Angelina Jolie was a knockout. When *Gia* premiered on HBO, *USA Today*'s Ed Martin wrote, "Jolie is dazzling as the doomed beauty . . . Her performance is a remarkably consistent mix of steely strength and crippling vulnerability. Jolie lays bare the real reason for Gia's eventual self-destruction: the exquisite pain of difficult relationships with her self-absorbed mother, Kathleen, and her frequently distant lesbian lover, Linda . . . Director Michael Cristofer dilutes the production somewhat with frequent filmic fluff. But overall, *Gia* is as hard to resist and as difficult to forget as its stunning title character and the woman who brings her briefly back to life."

Los Angeles Times reviewer Don Heckman was effusive. "Line up the Emmys, the Golden Globes, and the CableACE awards. Angelina Jolie's performance as the meteoric supermodel Gia Carangi in HBO's *Gia* stands up and demands attention as the work of an impressive young talent . . . In a role that takes her through a roller coaster of emotions, obsessions and addictions, Jolie is convincing throughout, the kind of performer whose central energy becomes the focus of every scene in which she appears . . . Like the character she is playing, she has the capacity to move past the cant and the artifice into the emotional heart of the drama."

"Nearly every scene reeks of a reality most of us will be lucky never to know," observed Michele Greppi of the *New York Post*. "With all due respect to writers, producers, director, and HBO executives, most of the credit for this must go to Angelina Jolie. She fearlessly, even recklessly, throws herself into every second. Every movement, every silence, every big, globby tear is a dare to everyone around her to keep up. The result is unforgettable." Ray Richmond of *Variety* called Jolie "a multifaceted revelation, shifting from coquettish to nasty to violent to contrite with a breathtaking believability. The passion with which

At a press conference for *Gia*

she inhabits the role is a spectacle in itself; it doesn't hurt that she's also a spectacular beauty."

Buoyed by her success, Angelina spoke euphorically about the woman whose character had initially left her cold. "I'd like to date her. I'd want to be her lover. In her pictures, when she was just hanging out, she had this little half smile, and she looked wild and wicked in a leather jacket. When she's free and just being herself, she's unbelievable; that's the tragedy of her story. You think, 'God, she didn't need drugs—she *was* a drug.'" *Gia* producer Marvin Worth was, in turn, enchanted by Angelina. "She is beautiful, and she is great—it's that simple," he told Steve Pond of the *Los Angeles Times*. "If she picks her next pictures right, I see her as a movie star, absolutely. Because she can do comedy, and she can do drama, and she can move."

But, just as her career seemed ready to explode, Angelina Jolie would contemplate walking away from it all.

SEVEN

THE NEXT BIG THING

Actors may crave the kind of roles they can sink their teeth into, but those fortunate enough to land a juicy part have to be prepared to make certain sacrifices. Some try to stay in character twenty-four hours a day so as not to lose their performing edge—a strategy that can alienate family and friends for the duration of the shoot. When the role has dark and disturbing aspects (and so many of the best ones do) the problem is compounded; the actor who takes on such a part may be troubled and distracted throughout the filming process and then require a postwrap decompression period. The role has stripped away layers of psychological self-protection, personal vulnerabilities have been exposed, and it will take time to recover. For example, Jessica Lange went through a period of depression after playing 1930s film star Frances Farmer, who was exploited by her mother and wrongly incarcerated in a mental institution. And Angelina Jolie felt similarly adrift in the months after *Gia* wrapped.

Things were going well for Jolie, the future looked bright, but, as she told *Playboy*'s Amy Longsdorf, "I was feeling emptier than ever. I was scared of going out like Gia. I needed to just get away and find myself again." To Jack Garner of Gannett News Service she confessed, "I'd really lost something. My brother told me once that when I was a little girl I was cute and had that sparkle in my eye. And I realized I had lost that sparkle. You just get hit by things in life."

Indicative of her malaise was her reaction to *Midnight Cowboy*, which she saw for the first time in 1994, at its twenty-fifth anniversary screening. "It moves you when you see your parents full of a certain ease and happiness when they were younger," Jolie said to *Newsday*'s Bob Heisler. "I feel I'm past that; I don't feel at ease, that kind of hopeful way of looking at life. To just enjoy life for me is very hard." To Peter M. Stevenson of *Mirabella* she added, "I walk around very convinced that I can be okay by myself. That I don't need anybody. I'm probably the last person to reach out and cry on somebody's shoulder, but I could probably use it."

Perhaps one trigger for Angelina's internal struggle was her sense that she was being compartmentalized by Hollywood and media power brokers. "The thing about this business, they like to stick you in one thing," she observed to Christine James of *Box Office* magazine. "And they like to tell you, 'You're the dark person,' or 'You're the sexy person,' or 'You're the mother, and you can't be something else.' You just have to keep fighting against it." She also revealed to Mimi Udovitch of *Rolling Stone* the same concern she'd mentioned to Longsdorf. After playing Gia, a woman with a glamorous public life and an impoverished private existence, she feared for herself. "I'd be working and doing interviews, and then going home by myself and not knowing if I'd ever be in a relationship or be really good in my marriage or be a good mother one day or if I'd ever be . . . I don't know, complete as a woman. It was a really sad time."

Angelina explained to Trish Deitch Rohrer of *Premiere* that she suffered inner turmoil because, "I became exposed at the same time that I was playing a role about somebody being exposed. I felt beaten down. I didn't feel like a good person. I felt pretty bad." Adding to the strain was the fact that her marriage to Jonny Miller was coming to an end. They both knew they'd married too young and were now growing apart, but they still clung to each other when times were tough. "Jonny came the day I 'died'" as Gia, Jolie said, "and he was with me when I shaved my head. We went home, and I still had all these glue spots, and I got into a dress and high heels, and he took me to dinner on Sunset Boulevard. He just went arm-in-arm with me into the restaurant."

Jolie with David Duchovny and Timothy Hutton

Jolie and her brother, James Haven, at the Academy Awards, 2000

Jolie and husband Billy Bob Thornton at the *Gone in 60 Seconds* premiere

Jolie poses with her father, Jon Voight, at ShoWest, 2000

Jolie at the 1999 National Board of Review Awards Gala

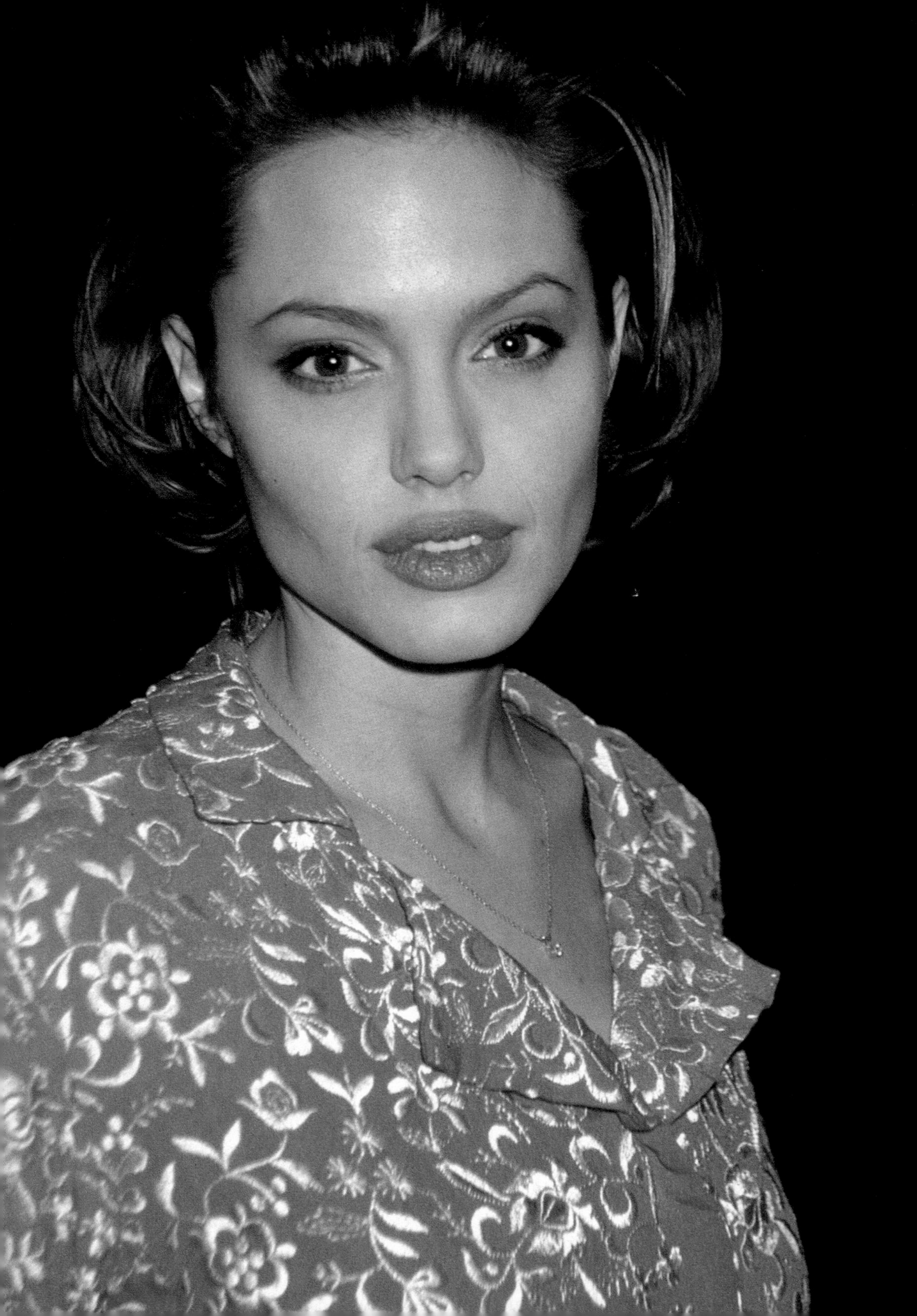

STEVE SANDS / OUTLINE

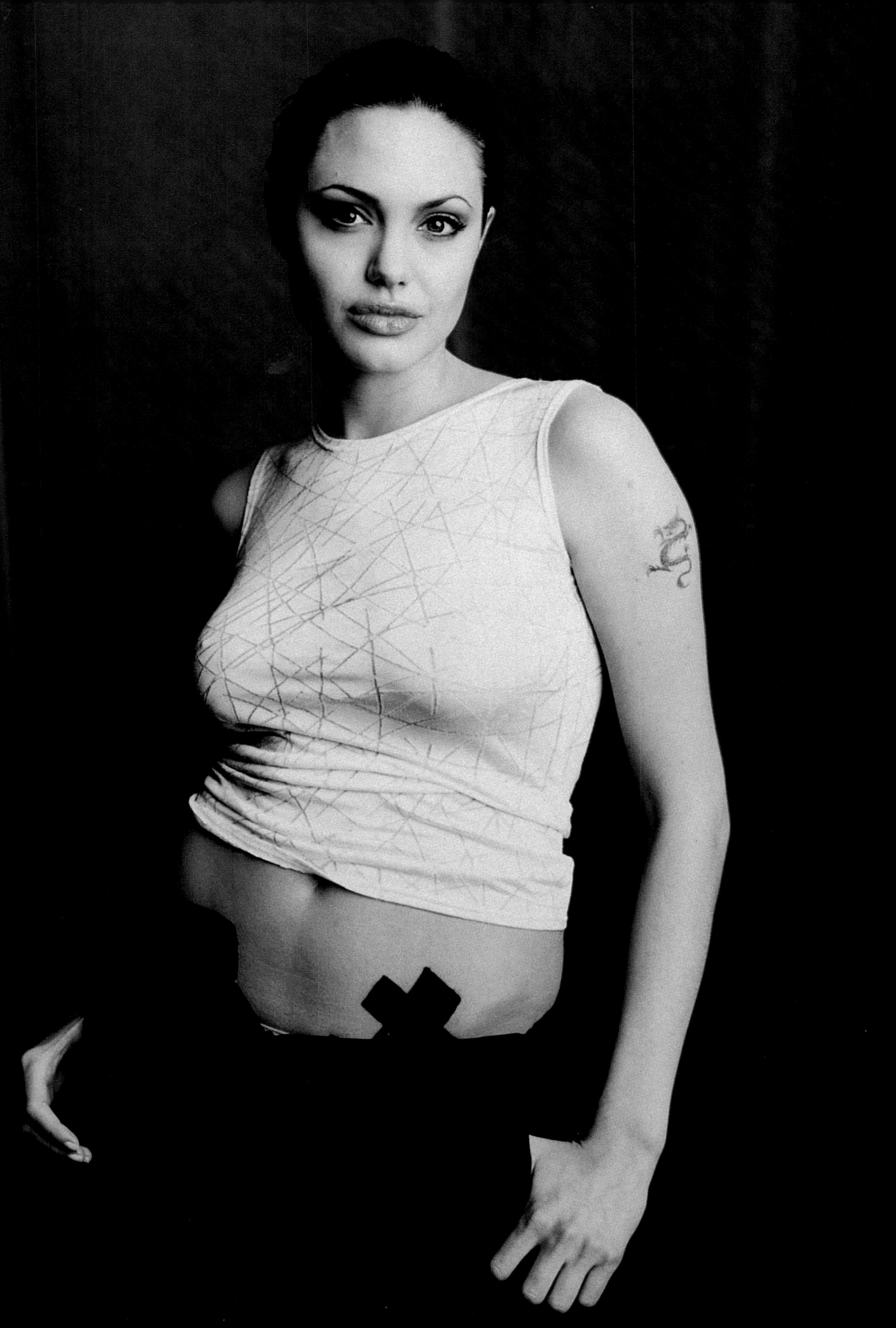

GEORGE HOLZ / OUTLINE

Jolie arrives at the 55th annual Golden Globe Awards, 1998

James, Angelina, and their father, Jon Voight,
at the 25th anniversary screening of *Midnight Cowboy*
BARRY KING / LIAISON AGENCY

But after *Gia* wrapped Angelina and Jonny split definitively, and
the combined emotional wallop threw Jolie completely off course. She
decided to quit acting—at least temporarily. Miller moved to London
and Jolie enrolled at New York University's film school with the idea of
reinventing herself and starting over. "I was pretty broken," she admitted to *Entertainment Weekly*'s Andrew Essex. "But it was very good for
me to get away after *Gia*, to not be in the spotlight, not have a chair.
Nobody was getting me a cappuccino in the morning. I was suddenly
on the subway with a backpack. Nobody knew me."

"I didn't know if I was gonna even be an actor anymore," she continued to Michael Angeli of *Movieline*, "didn't know if I would miss being an actor. There were lots of terrifying moments, lots of uplifting moments, but for a few months, which included spending a Christmas alone . . . being on the subway a lot . . . I was terrified of being on my own." Six months into her self-imposed exile Jolie reassessed her situation. She now realized how lucky she was to have been given the opportunity to learn on the job. Jolie told Christine James that John Frankenheimer had invited her to visit his film set—"he would show me lenses." Her alternative was to remain in New York and "sit in a classroom. So I don't think I'm going to go back [to school]." The recovery period was over.

Speaking to Angeli, Jolie articulated the lesson she had learned from all this: "It's important, in between projects, for me to sit down with who I've just become and allow her to continue to evolve and find a home inside me before I go and become somebody else. But I think I also need to learn to relax and not prepare too much, just enjoy life. I notice that my characters go out to dinner and have fun and take these great trips, but I spend so much time on their lives, I don't have much of a personal life of my own. I have to sort of remember to fill out that little notebook on me."

During her hiatus Angelina had also thought about whether she should alter her approach to the media. In a lengthy, almost surreal *Esquire* magazine profile of Jolie by John H. Richardson, the question of Voight's discomfort with the way his daughter bared her soul in interviews was raised. "I've talked about, you know, everything," said Jolie. "And just being really outspoken about my marriage and, you know, being with women, and they will take it and turn it into different things. So he's wanting me to kind of be quiet." To *Allure's* James Kaplan, Angelina confided that Voight had been talking to her recently about the issue. "I felt like explaining to him that when he was my age, the press was a little different. And you know, he's also not a young woman. So he can advise me however he wants, but they'll allow him to talk about things going on in Ireland and the Native American people and his process for his work. They don't ask me those things." Richardson also quoted her as saying, "A lot of people wanted me to be quiet during *Gia*, to not say if I'd ever done any drugs, or had ever slept with a woman, which to me was being totally hypocritical. If I had, and if I could identify with the story that much more, and really saw a beautiful thing in another woman . . . I didn't see why it was so bad."

Yet Jolie did understand the risks involved in opening her life wide to media scrutiny. She often felt that when she offered up the details of her private experience in an attempt to be honest with herself and her fans she was taken advantage of. To Kaplan she explained that she might talk about some of her teenage antics or her attraction to women, "because it's something I've learned about, and it's a beautiful thing. But [the media] just want to sell magazines. And they'll take a quick sound bite and make it a full article, which really does infuriate me, because nobody has learned anything."

Still, communicating with the media was a necessary part of her job; she had to promote herself as a public persona and promote the projects she was involved in—just like any other high-profile entertainer. And she could either do it fighting to conceal her true self every step of the way or approach it as a form of therapy. For Jolie the choice couldn't have been more straightforward. "I don't understand artists that don't communicate as much as I do, because in some ways it's saved my life," she commented to Barry Mann of Australia's NW magazine. "You can hide or you can go through things and talk openly. I feel nurtured by other people by shouting out my feelings, and, in doing that, I've got to know people on such a huge level." Of course, people got to know Angelina Jolie on a huge level, too.

The irony of it all is that in her pursuit of honesty Jolie created some false impressions. Because she was so frank in discussing her sexuality, some assumed that she was promiscuous, but Jolie insisted that when she married Jonny Miller he was only the second man she'd ever slept with. "I know I present myself as many things," she said to Mann. "I'm very sexual, yet I've always been monogamous." Then Jolie launched into some more of the kind of spontaneous self-analysis that endeared her to her interviewers. "I feel both masculine and feminine," she proclaimed. "I relate to the *hunter aspect* that most men have in their personalities, and the less maternal qualities. That's probably why most of my friends are men. I understand that side of men that encompasses the lone person. I have the restless spirit of a man." But this wasn't to say that Angelina lacked femininity. "I have fun putting on a

dress and walking down the red carpet. Sometimes, I'm *ridiculously female.*"

The Rolling Stones seemed to agree. They asked her to appear in their video for "Anybody Seen My Baby?" Afterwards Jolie described the experience as "amazing." She also loved meeting the Stones. "They're actually really nice people; they're each individually exactly what you would expect. They're really nice . . . meeting them was nice. Stripping for them, though, was really nerve-wracking, and I was scared." In the video Angelina exposes more than her love of music. "I was doing the job, and they said, 'Do a little act, and, like . . . run around the streets and Mick will chase you.' And I thought, 'Okay . . . um . . .' And then I got there and they said, 'You have this outfit and just get in front of them and do a dance and be sexy, and take it off.' And I nearly threw up." In fact Jolie didn't even consider herself a dancer. "Yeah, how much pressure is that?" she joked to *USA Today*'s Elizabeth Snead.

It was time for Jolie to get back to doing what she did best, so she signed a film contract. Her next project would be the romantic comedy *Playing by Heart*, in which she'd portray a young woman named Joan who craves love so desperately that she arranges to have her car stolen—this will oblige her date to spend more time with her. The role was quite a departure for her. "Sometimes I'm such a serious person," she admitted to Jack Garner of Gannett News Service. "Joan is so kooky and crazy, and so different from me. I didn't identify with it, but then I realized I liked it. It made me feel good to do weird things that made people laugh."

Playing by Heart was made on a modest budget of fourteen million dollars, and it included no car chases, no major explosions, no heroic rescues. Writer-director Willard Carroll fashioned his examination of love and loss, set in Los Angeles, from a set of six relationships that evolve over an eight-day period. "Suddenly it came to me," he remarks, "that I could connect a series of love stories that crossed different generations in a variety of situations: romantic love, maternal love, and even illicit love . . . So many books, poems and songs have been written about love in an attempt to find special ways to put into words feelings that are somewhat intangible. We've made a movie in which a variety of characters try to talk about love, a subject that affects everyone but is so difficult to talk about."

Although Carroll was a relatively unknown director he managed to assemble a stellar cast and crew to work on his film. Jolie costarred with the likes of Sean Connery, Gena Rowlands, Anthony Edwards, Madeleine Stowe, Dennis Quaid, Jay Mohr, Ellen Burstyn, Ryan Phillippe, Gillian Anderson, and Jon Stewart. Behind the camera was award-winning cinematographer Vilmos Zsigmond, who remarked to Bob Fisher of *American Cinematographer*, "This movie reminds me of my early days in Hollywood, when I did little pictures like *McCabe and Mrs. Miller*, *Cinderella Liberty*, and *Deliverance*. It tells a real story and recaptures the joy of filmmaking." For Jolie working with Zsigmond reinforced a sense of professional community and continuity: the cinematographer had worked with her father on *Deliverance* back in 1972. There really was a Hollywood filmmaking "family," and she belonged to it.

Carroll told Fisher that he'd wanted Zsigmond for *Playing by Heart* because, "I didn't want talking heads. I also wanted an elegant, romantic view of Los Angeles. It's a city we don't normally associate with romance. You can see the city in virtually every scene, and I felt that was important because I've seen too many movies where sets are practically screaming that they are fake." Added Zsigmond, "We discussed each character and couple, including the look and feel of their scenes and environments. When I worked with director Mark Rydell on *Cinderella Liberty*, the lighting style was a kind of 'poetic realism.' That's also what Willard wanted. It's prettier than reality, and serves the story better. If you are doing a Frankenstein movie or *Star Wars*, it doesn't have to be realistic—in fact, it should be more impressionistic or surrealistic. If you are telling a story about real people, the classical painters gave us a good model. They never lit anyone badly, and they never used soft light. They always had nice modeling light on the faces and darker backgrounds so the people would stand out."

It took forty-one days to shoot *Playing by Heart*, and during this time many of the actors involved never encountered one another. The movie was made up of vignettes and each actor only worked on a fraction of the whole. For example, Connery and Rowlands worked for eight days to complete their scenes, and Gillian Anderson put in eighteen days. Such a schedule is comfortable for the actors, but it's highly stressful for the director. "It was like starting another movie every week,"

Carroll explained to Fisher. "We shot for five days a week and rehearsed on the weekends with the couple that was starting the next week."

Like many of his fellow screenwriters Carroll created some of his characters with specific actors in mind. He'd envisioned Rowlands and Burstyn as Hannah and Mildred, and he was lucky enough to recruit them. Once those two respected names were attached to the project, casting the rest of the film was relatively easy. The budget was small, which meant that everyone had to accept a sizable pay cut (each actor was paid the same salary—fifty thousand dollars) and make do with modest trailers (on today's film sets trailer size is an indicator of star power). No one objected to making such concessions for the sake of the project. Connery even declined a driver, another standard perk, and drove himself to the set every day.

Playing by Heart was structured, as Carroll told *Daily Variety* columnist Army Archerd, "like a mystery—without a dead body." The mystery is, what is going to tie this disparate bunch of characters together, and the audience isn't let in on the secret until the film's final act.

Gena Rowlands and Sean Connery play Hannah and Paul. She is the host of a successful television cooking show, and he is her producer. It turns out that Paul is suffering from an incurable illness, but as the couple prepare to celebrate their fortieth wedding anniversary it's not the spectre of death that's creating shockwaves within their relationship—it's the revelation that Paul was once unfaithful to Hannah.

Gillian Anderson is Meredith, a theater director. She's been burned by love one too many times, and now she's a confirmed bachelorette. Her closest male companion is her dog, a 175-pound mastiff. He succeeds in keeping his mistress's would-be suitors at bay, until an architect named Trent comes along. Trent, played by Jon Stewart, is determined to win Meredith's heart.

We are first introduced to Hugh, portrayed by Dennis Quaid, when he shows up at a bar and claims to have been responsible for the deaths of his wife and child. Soon we learn that Hugh's pattern is to get drunk, introduce himself to a female bar patron, and spin a new version of his life story. He will eventually weave his romantic lies to the likes of Patricia Clarkson, Natassja Kinski, and drag queen Alec Mapa. Madeleine Stowe and Anthony Edwards are Gracie and Roger. Each is married to someone else, but they meet secretly to carry on a sex-with-no-regrets affair. Gracie's husband is the pathological Hugh, the inventor of tumultuous lives that divert him briefly from his own hollow existence.

Jay Mohr plays Mark, a hospital patient. Ellen Burstyn is his mother, Muriel, who is struggling to come to terms with the news that her previously married son is gay and he's dying of AIDS. In the few days Mark has left to live, he and Muriel attempt to repair their fractured relationship.

Angelina Jolie's Joan is a lonely young actress. Joan is in the process of breaking up with her boyfriend from a nightclub pay phone when she is smitten with Keenan, played by Ryan Phillippe. Although Keenan tries to keep Joan at arm's length, the two club denizens strike up a tentative romance.

While some industry insiders may have been surprised to see an A-list star like Connery become involved in a small, independent feature like *Playing by Heart*, the actor himself remarked, "I don't understand what all the fuss is about." Interviewed by Amy Longsdorf of Gannett News Service, he stated his reasons for accepting the part—reasons that should have been self-evident. The bottom line was the quality of the material. "I thought the guy in *Playing by Heart* was an interesting character. It really all depends on the writing, which is how it's always been for me. Even with my least successful movies, I liked the idea of the script to begin with. With *Playing by Heart*, I thought we had a chance to make a terrific movie, and I think we realized that during shooting." It didn't matter that the audience wasn't used to seeing Connery in roles like that of Paul. As Carroll told Longsdorf, "I admire him for wanting to play a man his own age. And I admire him for wanting to look like an old shoe."

Rowlands, the first to commit to the film, was the one who suggested in the first place that a script of *Playing by Heart* be sent to Connery. "I begged and begged for Sean to be in the movie," she said to Longsdorf. "When I heard that he had signed on, I couldn't have been more delighted. I've always wanted to work with him. We've known each other socially, which was nice. But, more important, we worked during the same period of time. I've seen his movies and I think he's seen at least one of mine. It does make a certain kind of relationship easy."

Comedian Jon Stewart was probably best known at that point as the host of Comedy Central's *Daily Show*. He was a newcomer to films when he took on the role of Trent, but the part's pop-cultural importance wasn't lost on him. To Joey Berlin of the *Washington Times*, Stewart cracked, "It took Duchovny five years to kiss [Gillian Anderson on *The X-Files*]—I did it in two weeks." But Stewart's most memorable *Playing by Heart* experience occurred after they'd shot a scene with the mastiff. In order to induce the dog to jump on the bed, the crew had smeared Stewart with chicken, but once the director yelled "Cut!" the beast kept licking Stewart vigorously. Finally, crew members were able to haul him off. "He wasn't a very seasoned actor," Stewart noted to Berlin. "Not like Lassie or Eddie." But Stewart wasn't complaining about the job; he considered himself lucky to have gotten it. "They were already shooting the film when I was cast," he claimed to online interviewer Prairie Miller. "It was one of those things where somebody must have dropped out. Or they got a case of food poisoning, or something. So they sent me the script and said, 'Do you want to run in and audition for this?' . . . It was sort of like winning a contest."

Starring opposite Jolie was Ryan Phillippe, who is inching his way towards young-leading-man status. Phillippe, who in real life is married to actress Reese Witherspoon, describes *Playing by Heart* as "a romantic mystery. Angelina and my characters are just pieces in a very complicated puzzle. It's one of the most ingenious scripts I've read, which is why I wanted to be a part of the project."

When a neighbor suggested that the teenaged Phillippe audition to act in commercials he thought it sounded like a good idea. At seventeen he moved to New York, and less than a year later he joined the cast of *One Life to Live*, becoming the popular daytime soap's first gay character. Two years later he relocated to Los Angeles, but he was disappointed to learn that he hadn't entered the land of milk and honey. "It was a rude awakening," he admitted to Louis Hobson of the *Calgary Sun*. "I had to struggle to get jobs. I did bit parts in episodes of *Due South* and *Chicago Hope* to pay the rent. I got so desperate that I did a terrible T.V. movie called *Deadly Invasion*, about killer bees. I grew a goatee and wore sunglasses in the hope casting directors wouldn't recognize me the next time I came to auditions." *Playing by Heart* was a big step forward for Phillippe.

For Jolie, *Playing by Heart* was a profile booster. When it was released the buzz about her took on a new theme: sure she had the looks and the talent to back them up, but she also appeared to have a knack for choosing roles that expanded her creatively. "I don't want to repeat myself," she declared to Garner, "not because I don't want to do similar movies, but because I'd already explored that side of myself and need to go somewhere else in my life. So I've been able to evolve through the characters. I've been very lucky to find characters at different times in my life that lead me in new directions."

Acting, for some, is a career, or even a means of acquiring wealth and fame; for others it's a calling, a vital form of personal expression. Jolie, of course, falls into the latter category. "I usually try to look for something I haven't done before, a side of me that I haven't completely explored," she said when *Playing by Heart* came out. "There's a truth in acting, and there is a very real part of me that can understand that or can believe in that or can see the beauty of that or see the ugliness in that and the statement that needs to be made. So it's kind of all me. But there are different sides of me that are harder." Her role in *Playing by Heart* was, "a very extroverted kind of personality who just had no darkness, really, and was just very, very positive, and wanting love, and kind of kooky and fun and up all the time and colorful . . . little short skirts and big huge monologues where she just goes on telling people stories and making faces. And for me, there is nothing in me that is normally like that or doesn't find it annoying. I had a hard time finding that rhythm in myself. But I eventually found it. Sometimes it's not the role but your one piece of a really beautiful puzzle." Overall, Angelina found Joan to be, "a beautiful person . . . because she wants to love and believe so much, and isn't shot down by the world and wary. She's just so hopeful. And I wanted to understand that side of me, and I wanted to answer the challenge."

In making this particular film Jolie seemed more in awe of her costars than she'd ever been before. "I can't even believe how I got into this cast with these people that I admire so much," she raved. "You're up there and you're trying to perform or trying to say something, and you're looking out and you're seeing Sean Connery, Gena Rowlands, Ellen Burstyn . . . and they're smiling at you, and they're so supportive, and you're just like, 'Oh my god! Oh my god! They're my heroes!' I

Angelina and her dad at the *Playing by Heart* premiere

was in the middle of doing a scene, and I looked over at Sean Connery and he suddenly smiled, and I just forgot what I was doing."

Momentary lapses such as that one aside, Jolie never lost sight of what made *Playing by Heart* meaningful. "It's the story of people that are unique and interesting to watch, but very human. Everybody will identify with somebody in it. And there are a lot of surprises in it. And it's sad and very real but it's also really colorful and fun to watch because there are so many people and so many different stories." Part of the film's value for Angelina was that it prompted her to think more carefully about the way she bonded with others. She remarked, "I've always had a tough time focusing on love or asking for love or asking someone to hold me. I'm not as much a romantic. I'm practical about things. I forget sometimes to look for that and be happy with that." Joan, however, is "free-spirited, and open, and a little crazy. But she's determined to make the important parts of life work. She's not distracted."

Playing by Heart premiered on December 10, 1998 at the Academy of Motion Picture Arts and Sciences. Jolie, clad in a pale pink jacket, was escorted to the event by her dad. Voight had come to the film set on Angelina's birthday, and he'd run lines of dialogue with her. Jolie charmed reporters on the night of the premiere, even performing an impromptu dance for the frenzied paparazzi. A bearded Voight, sporting a red bandana and a brown leather jacket, chatted amicably with the ladies and gentlemen of the press. He was obviously pleased to hang back and watch his daughter revel in the spotlight. "They're working her very hard, but she's doing wonderful work and getting attention for it," he commented to the *Toronto Sun*'s Jim Slotek. "She's not my little girl anymore. When I talk to her, I realize I'm talking to an extraordinary artist, somebody I can share things with." Voight also told *People* magazine that when he was working on *Varsity Blues*, "These young guys would come up to me and say, 'Oh, Mr. Voight, your work is so wonderful' . . . Baloney! It's all a big smoke screen! They just want to get to Angie."

The media now began singling Angelina Jolie out as The Next Big Thing. She, however, would not allow herself to get caught up in the hype. She kept insisting that it was all a mistake, it wasn't going to work out, she was an incorrigible misfit. Speaking to *Playboy*'s Amy Longsdorf, she asserted, "I'm one of the most flawed people. I woke up this morning and broke the phone by falling over." To Steve Pond of the *Los Angeles Times*, she confided, "Even though people respond more to my work now, they don't know what to do with me. There aren't too many roles like [Cornelia] Wallace and Gia out there. So it's not like I suddenly fit into all the regular movies. It's almost like I don't fit even more. I've proven that it's that much more complicated to have me just play the wife, or the mother—which I'd love to do, and I can."

Yet the critics felt that Jolie fit perfectly into *Playing by Heart* and helped to mitigate the film's shortcomings. Lisa Schwarzbaum of *Entertainment Weekly* wrote that the movie's "pairs of Angelenos wear their quirks so brightly, they might as well be dressed in safety orange. The entertainment, then, comes down to performances by hip actors enjoying their nicely lit parts. It's fun to see Anderson acting so self-destructively neurotic. It's neat to see Connery and pitch-perfect Rowlands purring and growling like the Lion King and Queen. And it's cool to see Jolie in anything, since, with her high-rising talent, she stands out like a skyscraper in this low-rise landscape." Although Andy Seiler of *USA Today* labeled the flick "Altman lite," he also wrote, "There are no bad performances in *Playing by Heart*," adding that Jolie turns in "a star-making performance."

Reviewer after reviewer heaped praise upon Angelina, and the tone of many was, "You heard it here first: A star is born." Buoyed by this fresh shot of professional and personal confidence, Jolie itched to take on new challenges and see where they might lead. "I can never stand still," she said earnestly to Louis Hobson of the *Calgary Sun*. "While I'm alive I'm going to move as quickly as possible and live as much as I can and I won't consider if that is good or bad for my career."

EIGHT

HER OWN KIND OF FUN

In January 1999, Angelina Jolie won her second Golden Globe. This time the honor was for her work in *Gia*. A few months earlier that role had snared her two Emmy nominations, but she'd lost out on both. It was clear that Jolie was still the darling of the Hollywood Foreign Press Association, though: she had two golden statuettes to prove it. Jolie's escorts to the awards ceremony on that January night were her soon-to-be ex-husband, Jonny Miller, and her brother, James Haven. The trio was in high spirits, and Angelina had vowed to some of her pals beforehand that if she won, she would do something wild and crazy.

The event was held at the Beverly Hilton Hotel. Jolie hatched the perfect plan. As teenagers she and some of her buddies had been kicked out of the hotel for jumping into the pool with their clothes on. So, after the awards had all been handed out, first Miller, then Haven, and finally Jolie, dove into the pool. Angelina emerged a moment later, dripping and smiling wide; she climbed out of the pool and posed happily for photographers. Her hand-beaded Randolph Duke gown was a soggy mess. What better way was there to launch a victory celebration? "To me it's funny that everyone isn't jumping in the pool," Jolie later commented to Bob Thompson of the *Toronto Sun*. "Because it's one of those nights. It's always surprised me that at one of those

At the 1999 Golden Globes

awards things, where there are wild people, free people, everybody is so serious, tamed by it all."

Untamed by success, Jolie went back to work. Appropriately, her career was soaring and she signed to do a film about air traffic controllers. Like many other films, *Pushing Tin* began as a magazine article. In 1996, the *New York Times Sunday Magazine* published an exposé called "Something's Got to Give," which looked at the high-pressure, anxiety-riddled microcosm of the New York Terminal Radar Approach Control (TRACON) center. In researching the article author Darcy Frey profiled several of the controllers who toiled in that intense atmosphere on a daily basis.

Hollywood producer Art Linson read the article and wasted no time in optioning the rights to it. "I read the piece and immediately thought it would be a great premise for a movie," he explains. "Darcy's article was funny, serious, and truly original. He captured the juxtaposition of the dramatic hazards of these guys' jobs with the comic energy of their personal lives and exposed the readers to a strange new world, a world we certainly have never seen on film before." From there Linson went on to hire the team of brothers Glen and Les Charles — writers and producers of the sitcom *Taxi* and cocreators of *Cheers*—to help turn the magazine piece into a movie script. Once the screenplay was completed, Linson and Laura Ziskin of Fox 2000 Pictures offered the script to British director Mike Newell, who was still basking in the glow of his 1994 hit *Four Weddings and a Funeral*. Newell had just finished making the crime drama *Donnie Brasco* with Al Pacino and Johnny Depp, and he needed a break. "I was tired," he recalls, "and I was by no means sure that I wanted to go back to work. But I took a look at the script, did some work with Glen and Les, and fell in love with them. They are two very inventive, receptive, and bright men . . . wonderful writers. I so enjoyed working with them that my involvement in the project sort of rolled on from there."

Newell describes what he and the Charles brothers finally came up with as, "a movie about people crashes, not plane crashes. It is a dynamic exploration of a high-stress work process . . . and work and stress are absolutely at the core of this story. I love that aspect of it because work and stress is universal. Everyone believes that their job is uniquely stressful. Whether you talk to an insurance salesman or a steelworker or a gardener, they all will tell you that what they do is more stressful than anything else. That idea, that everyone's job is stressing them to death, made me laugh. In the world of air traffic controllers, it is no different. It's a frantic, chaotic job in which there are enormous dangers and very disruptive energies. It's an outlandish, almost secret world that not many people know about. When you watch them work, organizing blips on a radar screen, controlling pilots and aircraft that don't really want to be controlled, you see that these guys are all silver-backed gorillas. They are all big alpha males . . . macho, dominant, messianic. There is not one of them who doesn't think that he's the biggest and the best. With that kind of attitude, you can see how superheated, dangerous rivalries could spring up all over the place if you get them positioned where one locks horns with another."

Another reason air traffic controlling is such a rich source of material for the screenwriter is the fact that the job, according to Newell, "starts to invade every aspect of [controllers'] lives, infecting their health, their marriages, and their minds. These guys are obsessed with, and terrified by their job at the same time. They have to find all sorts of escape routes in their emotional and psychological lives. The fallout of all this stress is where the drama, the gallows humor, and the morality tale come together in the story."

Pushing Tin revolves around the rivalry between two hot dog controllers, Nick Falzone and Russell Bell, a classic pair of alpha males. John Cusack and Billy Bob Thornton were signed to play them. "There are definitely similarities between John and Billy Bob and the characters they play," says Newell. "I wanted John from the very beginning. He is a master actor, theater-trained, and he can take a lot on his shoulders. I wanted him because he does have a kind of manic quality with a little-boy charm and innocence, which works well for Nick, who is constantly getting slapped by life. At every turn there is a custard pie in Nick's face and John's ability to be innocent in the face of life is a very funny thing." For Cusack, the role of Nick Falzone was a throwback to a time when ensemble films were popular. "When I first read the script it reminded me of Robert Altman's *M*A*S*H*. The backdrop is a place filled with a serious, unending threat of human casualty but the characters are full of comically endearing flaws and failings. Much like the army surgeons, if an air traffic controller screws up, people could die. I think it's that sense of impending doom that sets up the irreverence of these characters . . . the humor comes out as a release of all the stress they are constantly experiencing. So the rivalry with Russell is how Nick's stress manifests itself."

Prior to casting Thornton as Russell, Newell had met him socially, but when Thornton came in to audition the director "didn't recognize him at first." The chameleonlike screenwriter/actor quickly mesmerized Newell. "Here was this very slim creature who spoke with an extraordinary accent and I suppose what I really liked about him was that in every fiber of his being he is laconic. He speaks laconically, he looks laconically, he thinks laconically . . . and so you're never entirely sure when Billy Bob is serious or joking or quite how you're being affected by him. That is the most important quality in the character of Russell." Thornton himself describes Russell as a "Zen" character. "And that makes Nick crazy. The humor comes from the difference between the two guys. Nick is very out there . . . he's a fast-talking Italian guy from New York and Russell is an even-keeled weirdo from the desert. That's a pretty funny combination to have sitting next to each other at a radar scope while thousands of lives hang in the air."

While *Pushing Tin* hinges on the conflict between Russell and Nick, Newell believes the glue that binds the tale together is the performances delivered by the rest of the ensemble, notably Cate Blanchett and Angelina Jolie as the rival controllers' wives. "We were looking for remarkable creatures," the director told Susan Wloszczyna of *USA Today*. "The casting director and I looked at all the hot up-and-comers." Jolie was quickly hired to play Mary Bell, but Newell had trouble finding the right Connie Falzone. "I got tired of hearing people make excuses for her," he recalls. "Most of the young actresses had a lack of enthusiasm for being a simple housewife. They tried to dress it up. Then Cate came along, God bless her." According to Newell, what sold him on Blanchett was her assertion, "I want to give you the most meticulously observed happy Long Island housewife ever."

Once Connie was cast, everything else fell into place. Newell was thrilled with the talent roster: "I'm so devoted to the entire cast. They are a very talented, very odd, very ill-assorted bunch that works perfectly for the film. There is no safe average in the cast and no safe average in the film. They all are so wonderfully adept and full of technique and invention that I simply just let them go. I rode them with a very light rein because they were so magnificently inventive." Reflecting on Jolie, Newell adds, "She's an extraordinary-looking creature, like some weird, undiscovered orchid. She had that little-lost-bad-girl thing, which she brought to the part. There really wasn't much there on the page for her character, and she filled in the blanks. She's a brave, bold girl. I kept checking her age, thinking, 'Is she really this young to be this good?'" And Jolie thought Newell was pretty good, too, noting, "Mike is really good at letting his actors go a little crazy. He allowed us great input in getting these great characters to jump off the page."

Jolie sees Mary, who almost destroys Nick's marriage, as, "the bad girl who drinks a lot and is really sexy and really cool and sleeps around. But in the end, the woman who's with the children at home and supports the husband is the strongest. And all of my traits that could be considered the cool girl are really . . . I think she's really quite a pathetic character."

When *Pushing Tin* was made, both Jolie and Blanchett were hot commodities. Blanchett had received an Oscar nomination for her star turn in *Elizabeth*, and Jolie had scored the Golden Globes for *George Wallace* and *Gia*. Both actresses had the luxury to pick and choose their projects, and both agreed that what drew them to *Pushing Tin* was, for the most part, Newell himself. "Mike is an absolutely fantastic major general," says Blanchett. "He understands the balance between the comedy and the pathos and he was such a great audience for which to play."

Pushing Tin was shot in Toronto, and prior to shooting the film those members who were to play controllers were tutored by the film's two technical consultants, Thomas F. Zaccheo, who was profiled in Frey's article, and Sheila McCombe, a Toronto-based controller. "It's a stressful job, no doubt about it," Zaccheo maintains. "To the lay person, it looks like a video game. It's definitely not . . . there is no reset button in our job. Typically, it's fifty-nine minutes of boredom and one minute of sheer terror, and that one minute of sheer terror can destroy you for the rest of your life. That's basically why we are such a close-knit group of people. The camaraderie is essential. We give and take a good amount of ribbing with each other, too. We have to, because our other friends and family can't relate to what we go through on a daily basis."

The ribbing and the rivalry had to be contained within the increasingly tense relationship between Nick and Russell. Thornton, whose job it was to create and build one half of that complex relationship, came into the project with an impressive list of credentials. Over the previous several years he had been nominated for a Best Supporting Actor Oscar for his work in *A Simple Plan*, and he'd won a Los Angeles Film Critics Award and a Broadcast Film Critics Award for his supporting performance in *Primary Colors*. But it was his critically acclaimed 1996 film *Sling Blade*, in which he starred, and which he'd directed from his own screenplay, that placed Thornton in the Hollywood firmament. For his efforts, the Academy honored him with the Best Adapted Screenplay Oscar and nominated him for Best Actor. Still, as he told online interviewer Prairie Miller, he wasn't exactly being mobbed by fans in the street: "Like, I'll be standing in a coffee line, and someone really staring at me will come up and then ask for my autograph. And I'm like, thank God, you know?" This was actually fine by Thornton, who generally rejects the star mentality. So does costar Cusack, who said to Bob Thompson of the *Edmonton Sun*, "Everybody wants to canonize everything that comes out. I don't take the short term seriously. I'm more concerned about the long term, and the process to get there. I've been doing this for a while. I've seen the cycles. It's like every two years. Then every so often it's my turn to be the flavor of the month. But I realize the stars really have to be in alignment for a film to work." Newell had clearly found a good match when casting his male leads. The stars were in alignment.

As *Pushing Tin* begins, the following epigraph scrolls across the screen: "You land a million planes safely, and then you have one little midair and you never hear the end of it." That dry black humor sets the tone for the picture, which has intentional elements of an updated western. Nick "The Zone" Falzone is the best controller at TRACON, where he works the night shift. But his confidence is undermined when a new controller (from out of the West), Russell Bell, comes onboard. When Nick meets Bell's nubile young wife, Mary, he can't resist her and ends up cheating on his wife. Nick and Russell's every encounter quickly becomes charged by their spontaneous rivalry. Nick's life erodes. After Nick sleeps with Mary, Connie sleeps with Russell. The inevitable explosions occur, and eventually the dust settles.

Apparently the macho posturings of the script spilled over into life on the set. "There was a tremendous amount of top-dog, bottom-dog stuff as to who could do the job best, ad-lib better, get into the shot—incredible competition," Newell said to Raymond A. Edel of the *Record*. "They were constantly jockeying for position. Billy Bob would come in every morning and say that people were so pleased with his performance that they were increasing his money." One scene called for Russell to lose a game of one-on-one basketball to Nick, but when the cameras started rolling all bets were off. "Billy Bob just kept sinking shots while John stood there and watched."

All of this sounds like outtakes from a buddy picture. But *Pushing Tin* wasn't a buddy picture—nor was it a straight comedy, a relationship film, or an action flick. It defied easy classification, and this, as Newell informed David Gritten of the *Daily Telegraph*, prompted one Twentieth Century Fox executive to complain, "'The director's too clever.' What he meant was, I come from somewhere else, not America. That culturally I wasn't quite the thing." The film, Newell continued, was "both fish and fowl. That's precisely why I like it." Unfortunately, it's also precisely why some critics didn't.

A number of reviewers also criticized Newell for failing to incorporate into his screenplay some of the intriguing information that Frey had dug up for his article. Others found the plot convoluted and unwieldy. Still, *Pushing Tin* did garner its fair share of positive reviews. Wrote Stephanie Zacharek of *salon.com*, "Part of what makes *Pushing Tin* so pleasurable is the way its four major players—Cusack, Thornton, Blanchett, and Jolie—work the tension that pulls their characters together and pushes them apart. Individually and as part of the ensemble, each knows when to yank tight and when to give the line some play." Geoff Pevere of the *Toronto Star* also awarded the film kudos: "Indeed, one of the movie's masterstrokes is the way in which it pokes fun at male sexual competition without endorsing it. The girls in this movie are easily more on the ball than the boys are, and *Pushing Tin* is every bit as likely to make women chortle in sympathy as make men flinch with occasional embarrassment."

Again, Jolie was singled out for special praise. Commented Owen Gleiberman of *Entertainment Weekly*, "This is the first high-profile movie role for Angelina Jolie, and already it's clear that she's that rare thing, a sex bomb who is also a major actress. In *Pushing Tin*, Jolie brandishes her bangs, her crooked bee-stung pout, and her tawny ripe body with seductive abandon, yet she also makes Mary a wounded, insidious basket case."

In the summer of 1999, the sex bomb/major actress suddenly found herself the darling of the magazine world. Her face adorned the covers of mainstream publications on what seemed like a monthly basis. Typically, Jolie downplayed the phenomenon, telling Francine Parnes of the Sydney, Australia *Daily Telegraph*, "You get a couple of big movies so they put you on magazine covers. People talk about you and the hype gets back to the studios and they decide they can capitalize on your sudden celebrity. It doesn't mean I'm a better actress than I was when they didn't want me in their pictures. It just means that people recognize my name and that makes me a viable commodity."

Jolie was perhaps being too modest. The reality was that models were being nudged off covers throughout the publishing industry. The most recent crop of supermodels, including those whom Parnes identified as the "deified six"—Cindy Crawford, Naomi Campbell, Linda Evangelista, Christy Turlington, Claudia Schiffer, and Kate Moss—had lost a certain amount of their cachet. And the next crop had yet to ripen. Parnes also reported that in January 1999 a leading fashion editor, Linda Wells of *Allure* magazine, had caused a stir by announcing to the *New York Times* that "Nobody cares about models anymore." *Allure* appeared to prove Wells's point: in 1998 it had a cover ratio of ten models to two celebrities; in 1999 that ratio was reversed. "I'm gambling on this, and it's an important gamble," said Wells, who then went ahead and put Angelina Jolie and Julianne Moore on two spring covers. "We are putting a lot more celebrities on the cover because I believe they will sell more. After all, that's what we're trying to do, sell magazines."

Busy demonstrating that she could sell magazines and movie tickets by doing what came naturally, Jolie was at the top of her game. The task of selecting a new project had never seemed more challenging and interesting. She applied herself to it, and as a result said yes to *Gone in 60 Seconds*, *The Bone Collector*, and *Dancing in the Dark*. And she said no to *Charlie's Angels*.

Sporting her new tattoo at the Bollywood Awards in London

Charlie's Angels was to be a high-profile Columbia Pictures project based on the seventies T.V. series of the same name. But it wasn't Angelina's cup of tea, despite wire-service reports that she had joined Drew Barrymore and Cameron Diaz by signing to play an angel. Columbia Pictures chairwoman Amy Pascal was clearly disappointed, calling Jolie, "a female James Dean for our time. I'd make any movie with her in it. I begged her to do the film version of *Charlie's Angels*. But she's no angel."

Explaining her decision to Louis Hobson of the *Ottawa Sun*, Jolie said, "When they sent me the script for *Charlie's Angels*, they said there were three reasons I should do it. They said there hadn't been really good, strong roles for women; that it would make me a big star; and that I would have a fun time doing it." Angelina begged to differ. "All my roles . . . have been strong female roles. The idea of being a big star has absolutely no appeal to me." Plus she had already committed to herself to costar in the remake of *Gone in 60 Seconds* with Nicolas Cage. "That was going to be my fun movie and I was going to have fun doing it with guys." Although Jolie did admit to Hobson that she found the *Charlie's Angels* script "cute and clever," she also pointed out that "Drew Barrymore and Cameron Diaz are already celebrities and they're going to have great fun spoofing their images with *Charlie's Angels*. I'm not at that point in my career, so audiences won't have as much fun watching me run around in high heels chasing bad guys and flipping my hair."

Angelina's notion of fun was something quite different. She would have fun doing *Gone in 60 Seconds* "with the guys," and she'd had a great time with *Pushing Tin*. She told Hobson in the *London Free Press* that *Pushing Tin* was, "probably the most fun I've had making a film. I started working on it right after I'd just come out of my dark period. I was really happy on the set. I loved my character and all the people on the set were such fun to be around. I really understand the whole theme of the film, which is dealing with your personal demons and with fear. It's what my whole life has been about. If I hadn't put a few of my demons behind me, I don't think I'd have felt as secure and happy as I did working on *Pushing Tin*."

One of the fun people on the *Pushing Tin* set was Billy Bob Thornton, Jolie's on-screen husband. In fact, he was a good deal more than fun; Jolie had begun to regard him as a kindred spirit. She was ready for a serious romantic relationship—she hadn't had one since her breakup with Miller—but Thornton (who had been divorced four times) was heavily involved with actress Laura Dern. So Jolie held back and let things develop at their own pace.

NINE

DARK THINGS

During interviews Angelina Jolie has often commented that she likes "dark things." She must have enjoyed making *The Bone Collector*, based on the best-selling thriller novel by Jeffery Deaver. The Universal film featured Jolie as a street cop who teams up with a quadriplegic detective named Lincoln Rhyme, played by Denzel Washington, to catch a vicious killer who is creating mayhem in Manhattan (or Montreal-as-Manhattan—the film was shot on location there). The cast also included Queen Latifah as Rhyme's caregiver, Thelma; Ed O'Neill as Detective Paulie Sellitto, Rhyme's former partner; and Luis Guzman as forensics genius Eddie Ortiz.

Rhyme, a forensics specialist who was once the country's leading criminologist, has a sharp eye for details, and his instincts have made him a legend within the law-enforcement community. He's also a best-selling author. Four years before the story opens he suffered a near-fatal injury in the line of duty and his life was torn apart—trying to rescue a wounded cop in a subway tunnel, Rhyme was struck by falling debris. He was left paralyzed and has since had little will to live. Meanwhile, a young, smart, but disillusioned rookie policewoman, Amelia Donaghy—played by Jolie—is being overwhelmed by the pressures of her work on the streets. On the eve of being assigned to a desk job, she discovers a horribly mutilated corpse.

Realizing that they're up against a particularly virulent form of evil, Rhyme's detective colleagues try to convince him to help them solve the crime; despite his physical handicap Rhyme still has the best criminal mind in New York. At first Rhyme refuses, claiming that he has no interest in some run-of-the-mill murder investigation, but after looking at the physical-evidence file and the crime-scene photos Rhyme agrees to become involved. He pulls a reluctant Donaghy away from her safe new desk job and makes her his ears, eyes, and legs in the field. Before long the two come to understand that they are pitted against a serial killer. This monster taunts Rhyme and Donaghy by leaving arcane clues for Donaghy to unearth and Rhyme to unravel—in what just may be enough time to save the next victim's life. As they work together to stop the killer Donaghy and Rhyme find themselves drawn closer and closer together, both professionally and personally.

Jeffery Deaver has described Rhyme as a "C-4 quad"; that is, he was injured at the fourth cervical vertebra and can only talk, nod, shrug, and move his left ring finger. "The kind of book I try to write is an emotional experience, very fast-paced, a page-turner," Deaver said to William F. Nicholson of *USA Today*. The author also claimed that his character's physical impairment allowed him to explore "some of the issues about who we are in the perfect-body cult of today's society. And what we are really, in essence, we are our minds. I wanted to create a character that was basically pure mind, an accomplished mind, as worthy and as savvy as the classic, mobile detective."

The film's producer, Martin Bregman, boasts a long list of credits, including *Dog Day Afternoon*, *Scarface*, *Sea of Love*, *One Tough Cop*, and *Serpico*. Knowing an effective suspense story when he reads one, he recognized instantly that Deaver's book would translate well into a film. "It's exciting and very scary," Bregman says. "It's also a love story, but a very different and strange love story. It has many elements that I have never seen put together in this way, and it deals with a heroic figure [in a way] that has never been done." In addition to hiring screenwriter Jeremy Iacone, Bregman brought director Phillip Noyce aboard. Noyce explains that he was attracted to the project because he saw it as four stories in one: "It's a love story. It's a thriller. It's a detective story. And it's a story of renewal and resurrection. Two people have lost themselves and given up; they find each other and, ultimately, the will that had failed them."

For Jolie the subtle romance that grows between Rhyme and Donaghy was a big draw. In fact, it was magical. "In other movies you'd have dinner-date scenes and sex scenes," she says. "Denzel and I had days of scenes where I'd have to help him move something or show him something or give him some juice. And when we'd talk we'd have to look at each other. He couldn't hold me . . . so his character was more connected to me sensually. The slightest touch was electric. It doesn't hurt that Denzel's a stunning and intelligent man and a very powerful presence." Noyce adds his own assessment of that relationship: "The first time Angelina and Denzel met she had almost a shyness with him, and I knew that she was going to transfer that shyness to her character. For a person who has a reputation for being quite complex, she's a very simple young woman in terms of the way she works with people. Her approach is very straightforward."

Elaborating on the special connection between Rhyme and Donaghy, Jolie told Louis Hobson of the *Calgary Sun* that she found the idea that this young policewoman could fall in love with this shattered, brilliant man totally believable. "I think the attraction is a beautiful thing and a possible thing. It certainly is for me, because I genuinely see past things like physical deformity, color, race, and sex. To me attraction is an aura thing. It's an energy given off by the other person that you react to or you don't."

His creative team in place, Bregman put his energies into casting the film. It was a difficult undertaking. Comments Bregman, "There are not many actors in their early forties that have the ability to play Lincoln Rhyme . . . you can count them on three fingers. We needed an actor, and hopefully a movie star, and were lucky enough to get both in Denzel Washington." Bregman adds that he was amazed at the way Washington, who had won the Best Supporting Actor Oscar for *Glory*, delved into the role. It had been "a joy to watch him work and prepare, and he brought something to this film that I'm not sure any other actor could have brought, which is a sense of reality and a tremendous intelligence."

Washington himself was pleased to take part in *The Bone Collector*.

With costar Denzel Washington at the New York premiere of
The Bone Collector

SEAN ROBERTS / EVERETT COLLECTION

He found the story gripping and saw the chance to play "a person who is quadriplegic [as] a great challenge for any actor. An actor's body is his instrument, and to have ninety-three percent of that taken away, you have to sort of act with your soul. I mean, they say the eyes are the window to the soul." But as he prepared to begin shooting the movie, Washington discovered that his role was even more demanding than he'd first imagined. "I've played some challenging individuals and parts in my days, but this was the most unique challenge, certainly physically. I've never had my tools taken away from me, the ability to express and move and turn my head as much as I wanted or to run or walk or laugh from the stomach, not just from the chest up. I definitely appreciate and have a better understanding, to a degree, of what quadriplegics must go through." Noyce fully appreciated how daunting the actor's task was: "Because he can't move, it's got to be the voice, the eyes and the mind that's seen working. He's playing a very intelligent guy who has been robbed of other faculties. He can't move and so we needed a truly great actor, and Denzel is one of the world's greatest."

Not surprisingly, an army of young actresses longed to be cast as Amelia Donaghy, Rhyme's ears, eyes, and legs. "We were looking for a very specific actress," explains Noyce. "She had to be young, in her mid-twenties, with the strength to play a New York cop, as well as a very special vulnerability. The character is really the heart of the story. She comes into the life of the character played by Denzel Washington and reignites his will to live. What I saw in Angelina's performance as Gia was all those qualities; the strength and the vulnerability, and also a fearlessness, both in the character she portrayed and—I realized when I met her—as an artist." Noyce is convinced that the same openness that gets Jolie into trouble during interviews is the essence of her acting. "She's very courageous as an actress," he remarked to Anne Bergman of the *Los Angeles Times*. "Angelina will go anywhere, or at least she'll try going anywhere that the director suggests. In addition, she has no pretension about herself, no airs." This is why producer Bregman so readily maintains that "After we saw Angelina Jolie's work in *Gia* and *George Wallace* there was nobody else we wanted. Nobody was as exciting as she was. Angelina may be the best actress to come down the pike in maybe the past twenty years."

Struck by the dichotomy between Jolie's on-and-off-camera selves, Noyce commented to Jeffrey Ressner of *Time*, "Porcelain isn't fine enough to describe how fragile she is. She's not burned out with the joy of performing. She's in her element because she can set parameters for a character, whereas I suspect she doesn't know her own boundaries emotionally and physically. I suspect she's happiest when she's not being Angelina Jolie."

It's interesting that Rhyme's physical limitations also restricted Jolie as Amelia. "It subdues your movement when you're with someone who can't move," she explains. "I naturally didn't . . . move out of his eyeline. You find yourself being stuck." Technical difficulties aside, Jolie was thrilled to be working with Washington. "He's brilliant and he's fascinating. He's obviously extremely good-looking, and he has this smile. You know, the first time Denzel smiled at me I think I blushed. I couldn't turn away, and he couldn't come running, so I just had to stand there. When he looks at you, he looks right through you." Washington himself is happy to turn it into a mutual admiration society. "Angelina's a wonderful actress," he says. He then recalls the day he first heard that she was up for the role of Amelia. "Marty and Phillip called and said, 'We've got this girl, you've got to see her. You're going to love her. She's great.' And they were right."

In fact, according to Jolie, Washington had approval over who his costar would be. To her relief, "after they showed him my work, he agreed to meet me to see if the chemistry was there. I was so excited he liked my work enough to sit down with me. I also thought he would be perfect for the role. It wasn't just that he's a great actor; I could really see him as this man. I don't think there are many actors that could be that still and have that kind of presence. I never thought about the race issue at all. But it's a great thing that it's in there and is not made into an issue."

As it turned out, Washington's approval of Jolie's participation in the project was just the final step in a long, contentious process. Universal Studios brass, Noyce explained to Andrew Essex of *Entertainment Weekly*, had initially insisted upon hiring a more "established" name to play Donaghy, but Noyce and Martin Bregman stood firm for Angelina. "When you see a film like *Gia,*" Noyce later told James Kaplan of *Allure,* "you recognize that Angelina has both technical ability and guts; she was willing to put herself out there. There was a lot of naked-ness in that picture, and she didn't shy away from it. Our script didn't call for nudity, but for her to bare herself emotionally that was crucial in our wanting to cast her." And in press notes Bregman recalled, "I had a similar problem with Michelle Pfeiffer in *Scarface.* Nobody knew who she was. But Angie's enormously gifted, and I usually get what I want." Still, stand-offs take time to resolve themselves, and all that Jolie could do was wait. "It took months," she told Essex. "I had to basically wait and wait and wait and beg and not take another job. But I don't blame them—I'd certainly never had a moneymaking film. They took a big risk."

While Jolie could accept the reasoning behind Universal's desire to cast a bigger name opposite Washington, she was rankled by the studio's concerns over race. "They questioned the interracial thing, since Denzel and I play two people who are obviously attracted to each other. I heard that and I thought it was a joke." All of these issues were at last ironed out, and it did indeed appear that Bregman had gotten his way—but at a hefty price. Universal forced him to lop twenty million off the film's budget (reducing the figure to forty-five million), and he had to guarantee that if they ran over budget, the difference would come out of the filmmakers' pockets. Noyce himself put up a million dollars because, as he says, "there was no one else."

Characteristically, Angelina didn't simply take the role when it was finally offered, count her blessings, and shut up. Once she'd committed to the project she had a few objections to make. First, the script called for Amelia to have been a model prior to joining the force. "I tried desperately to get that out of the script," Jolie told Sherri Weiner of *UniverCity Magazine*. Second, Jolie objected to Amelia having a sex scene early in the movie. "I didn't feel it was necessary to show her sexuality," she continued to Weiner. "I thought it needed to be about her work. But the filmmakers thought that if they showed that she didn't enjoy sex [in that scene], then it would somehow translate to her being with someone who was quadriplegic. I thought none of that needed to get introduced." Jolie won that round and then took a third stand; the filmmakers wanted her to don a little red party dress for the last scene of the film, and she balked. She envisioned a long, elegant number, something "simple and classy," to harmonize with Rhyme's tuxedo. "The reality of her standing next to him in the wheelchair and having a short, little dress on was ridiculous."

As these details were being negotiated, Jolie immersed herself in her new role. *The Bone Collector*'s premise and development hooked her and reeled her in. When she first read the script Jolie had come down with a serious case of the creeps. "I was alone in my apartment and it scared me to death. I couldn't stop reading [the script], and I couldn't forget about it when I put it down, which says a lot to me. It kind of haunted me." But what haunted Angelina most persistently was the screenplay's emotional core: the relationship between Rhyme and Amelia. "To me, theirs is one of the most beautiful relationships, if not the most intense love story I've ever done, because it was really based on their believing in each other—their minds and their instincts and their souls. There was nothing physical. It got to me when I first started to hear it, when I was alone in those rooms and I would hear his voice saying, 'I'm here. I'm here for you' . . . We all find ourselves in our life completely alone somewhere, when only we can take care of ourselves in that moment and nobody else is there to help us, and suddenly you hear the voice of somebody say, 'I'm here for you and I'll be with you every step of the way.' That's like the greatest thing you can possibly imagine."

Speaking to Weiner, Jolie reflected on how playing Amelia Donaghy had crystallized her understanding of the true nature of love. "There are very few people that can hold me, that I can talk to about my life and can make me cry. There are few people who I'd want to come to and say, 'Look at what I did.' So I can have sex with anyone, but there's hardly anyone to share things with. I've only had a few partners, a handful, in my life. [Playing Amelia] changed my view of relationships. Anybody in my life at the time—if I was seeing someone or talking to someone, if they only wanted to be with me for that kind of sexuality—it wasn't enough. If they weren't interested in my work and how I was feeling, then it didn't come close to what I was experiencing at work on the set."

As Jolie set about inhabiting the character of the young policewoman, she was deeply gratified that Donaghy was no stereotype. She later observed, "So many of the women in film are angry or not very feminine. Luckily she was all of that and strong as well. She was a very well-rounded character and had a great arc—she discovered her own strengths and purpose as she went along." Jolie could thank Deaver and Iacone and, especially, Noyce for that. Noyce was determined to build strong, authentic personas for both Donaghy and Rhyme. In order to make Rhyme—who can only control the movement of one finger—as believable as possible, the director researched the treatment of quadriplegia, which really didn't start in earnest until after World

War II. "Prior to that time," says Noyce, "once you severed your spinal cord it was really the end; but, increasingly, it has become the beginning of another life—a completely different one, but not the end of living." Before filming started Noyce and Washington met with some leading spinal cord specialists at New York's Mount Sinai Hospital and several hospitals in the Los Angeles area. Washington also got together with over a dozen quadriplegics, including actor Christopher Reeve, who was paralyzed after being thrown from a horse.

Queen Latifah, who plays Rhyme's nurse, Thelma, also had a chance to talk with Reeve, who has become one of America's most outspoken spinal-research activists. Latifah recalls "feeling inspired" by their meeting. "Christopher has a lot of love for what he does. He understands his situation, has hope, a positive attitude, and he's able to share that with other people in the same situation, and that's important." To enhance her understanding of Thelma's world, Latifah met with a number of nurses and caregivers, as well. She used the opportunity to learn more about "what kind of injury Rhyme had, and what kind of care he needed. There is no person more intimate with a quadriplegic than his caregiver, because she sees the ups and downs and good and bad of everything. You can use your imagination as to what a person would need to do for you when you can't do almost anything for yourself that requires movement. So they have a really close relationship. It's important from a technical side, but also from the human side of it. It's hard for someone who wants to be alone but can't be. So we played the relationship as comfortable, as though we were both used to the situation."

The filmmakers had to strive for accuracy in other areas, too. Before committing scenes from *The Bone Collector* to film, says Bregman, they had to do some heavy research into methods of police work. They consulted a range of specialists and brought in Detective Hal Sherman of the Forensics Investigation Division of the NYPD to serve as the film's forensics consultant. Insists Bregman, "There's a reality in this film that you very seldom, if ever, get. It's been thoroughly researched and is a very accurate depiction of this world we've filmed." Jolie herself examined stacks of crime scene photographs and reports. "I went to actual forensic labs here in New York and saw pictures of things that had happened not far away from where I live; things that happen every day in New York. They were things that were so brutal that I never knew somebody could do to another person. I never saw anyone beaten to death by a tree branch or burnt to death before. But I had to do it to know what my reaction would be. You can't swallow, your mouth drops open and you just feel your guts empty. It's not emotional—it's a physical reaction."

But Jolie admits that beyond the horror lies a certain fascination. "All of a sudden you see chipped nail polish, and you realize that a week ago this woman had a life. You see stretch marks and you realize this woman was beaten to death by her husband who she had children with at some point. You see a mother and daughter burnt to death as they were running together and you can hear their screams." Eventually this leads to a determination to interpret the physical evidence and use it to apprehend the person who has destroyed these lives: "You go past that and see the blood spattered in a certain way and you want to get the guy that did it and find the evidence. In my character there's that duality—half of [Amelia] is weak and she needs to become a stronger person in order to catch the guy."

Jolie discussed some of her other preparations for the project—such as meeting with real policewomen—in her interview with Weiner. She explained, "I met a lot of them and they were actually stronger than I thought Amelia should be. A lot of the policewomen I met were a lot tougher than the men. They made a decision to be what they needed to be. They were, like, dead serious. I think they felt the need to keep that authority in order to be respected. I just didn't think Amelia was like that. She was only on the force a few years. They say when you're on the force a few years or [heading] towards retirement, those are the times you're the most vulnerable and can commit suicide. Many cops do—their gun is right there. People joined the force because they thought they could change the world and then they see that they can't. You see these trials go on and you don't have that extra piece of evidence. You know he's guilty and you see him walk . . . And every day you see poverty. That's what happened to Amelia. She's sickened by people and the world and doesn't feel she can do anything about it. That's why she wants to go behind a desk and get off of the streets."

Finally the highly prepared cast of *The Bone Collector* was ready to start filming. There to lead them through their difficult paces was

Noyce, who quickly earned their respect and admiration. Washington gave the director credit for teaching him "a lot about shooting film and understanding what a motion picture is, and how to tell a story cinematically . . . he's excited about every shot, and about every take, and that's rare. It's really wonderful to see, and it inspires me." Jolie liked the fact that Noyce could see things from a female perspective. "It takes a certain kind of a man to appreciate and really understand the type of woman Amelia is and all the different sides of her. And Phillip knows and identifies with her soft side, and he gets her when she's strong. He knows it's complicated, and he's just as baffled by her and just as open to whatever comes out of me—it might be just what's right for her so we'd try a hundred things because she's not an easy person to figure out." It was an entirely reciprocal relationship, because for Noyce it all depended upon the actors. "Everything else follows the performance," he asserts. "That's the cake, and the cinematic flourishes become the icing on the cake." But, given that *The Bone Collector* is a film with a virtually motionless character at its center, applying those flourishes was a lot more difficult than frosting a cake. As Noyce explains, the specific challenge they faced was to prevent things from becoming static. While much depended upon the dynamism and subtlety of the actors' performances, the camera also had a vital role to play. "We could have artificially moved the actors, but I decided not to do that and let them play the reality instead. We also could have artificially moved the camera, but I decided not to do that either because each camera move needs to be motivated by something within the scene. In fact, the only time the camera moves in a shot involving Rhyme is when he's talking to Amelia via radio and she's moving, working a crime scene on his behalf. We shot twice as many camera setups and camera angles as you would for a normal dialogue scene, so that when the scene is cut the audience will get the impression of kinetics or movement simply because the camera is always cutting to somewhere new, and we hope to always be one step ahead of the audience."

The Bone Collector was released in November 1999, and it represented a major career milestone for Jolie: it was the first time her name had ever appeared above the film's title. "I fell over laughing when I found that out," she confided to Bob Thompson of the *Toronto Sun*. "I have never been above the title. I've never been in a big movie. So I'm excited. It's also weird, because I'm not so sure about myself as a police officer. I play a police officer. To be launched in a role like that is really frightening. I'm the one with the gun and the walkie-talkie and the flashlight. And I'm thinking, 'I look like I'm five years old.'" She just couldn't seem to get over this profile elevation, telling *Paris Match*'s Dany Jucaud that just before *The Bone Collector* opened she happened to be driving down Sunset Boulevard in Los Angeles and spotted an ad for the film. "I noticed my face next to Denzel's on a huge billboard [and] I almost had a car accident. I thought I was dreaming."

In advance screenings of *The Bone Collector* audiences responded warmly to Angelina. The critics tended to respond in the same way. In fact most reviewers gave the entire cast top marks. For example, *People* magazine enthused, "Restricted to acting mostly from the neck up, Washington manages to create a vivid portrait of a complicated man who is alternately depressed, self-mocking, and obsessed with his job. The talented Jolie, all sharp edges and attitude, proves a worthy match."

It must have all seemed familiar to Jolie, however. Again, the tenor of most reviews was praise for individual performances but disappointment in the film as a whole. Philip Wunch of the *Dallas Morning News* took issue with what he considered the movie's one-dimensional bad guy. "It's a nondebatable cinematic fact that a thriller is only as thrilling as its villain. Yet everyone connected with *The Bone Collector* . . . must have forgotten that truism. Denzel Washington is fine, Angelina Jolie is more than fine, and Phillip Noyce's direction is frequently astute. But the film's impact is dulled by the lack of emotional investment in the villain. When the heinous being is finally revealed, you'll shrug and think, 'So what?'" Bruce Fretts of *Entertainment Weekly* opined that the film would have veered into kitsch had it not been for Washington. "Without him, some of *Collector*'s more far-fetched plot twists (of which there are a few) might have received a less-welcoming response." (Interestingly, Noyce himself supported this contention when he said, "In one scene we had [Washington] off screen asking Angelina to cut off the hands of a female murder victim. For two test screenings we had sniggers in the audience—unease. So I asked the editor to put Denzel on screen—dead silence. His authority made it okay.")

Despite the lukewarm and occasionally negative notices it received, *The Bone Collector* was in no way down for the count. It actually turned

At the Screen Actors Guild Awards, 1999

out to be one of those films that remains unaffected by its bad press and goes on to achieve commercial success. Grabbing the number-one-at-the-box-office spot the week it opened, the film went on to earn an estimated $17.2 million to date, and it further cemented Angelina Jolie's status as a star who could "open" a film. However, it was her next movie that would finally vault her into the ranks of Hollywood's new royalty.

TEN

"DO YOU BELIEVE WE'RE HERE AND THEY LET US IN?"

Girl, Interrupted is one of those projects that endured what Hollywood insiders call "development hell." Producer Douglas Wick, who steered *The Craft* onto the big screen and helped make Neve Campbell a star, first optioned Susanna Kaysen's book of the same name in 1993. A short time later Winona Ryder became attached to the project as both star and producer, putting it on what is referred to as "the fast track." But after scripts submitted by three different writers failed to make the cut, *Girl, Interrupted* was relegated to the back burner.

Desperate to resurrect the project, Ryder approached director James Mangold, who had just finished filming *Copland*. "I was unsure about getting involved," Mangold admitted to Tricia Lanie of *Entertainment Weekly*. "I thought everyone wanted a Lifetime movie—weepy girls in smocks, all retching and twitching. I said, 'I want to make a monster movie,' a movie about what it's like to lose your boundaries in your world." Elsewhere Mangold reflected, "Women get ripped off because movies geared towards them are all so fuzzy and pastel and *The Way We Were* squared. I wanted to bring some of the edge of my other movies to this one, which is, naturally, going to be construed as a chick flick. That was the challenge—to give a women's film some cojones."

It's hard to fathom why so few people involved in something as neurotic and imbalanced as the entertainment industry would be able to figure out how to do justice to a book like *Girl, Interrupted*, which chronicles Kaysen's nearly two-year-long experience in a mental institution. What landed her there was a halfhearted suicide attempt—she washed down a bottle of aspirin with a bottle of vodka—but for some time she'd been a worry to her Boston blueblood parents due to her inappropriate behavior. Kaysen had nodded off during her high school graduation ceremony and been extremely apathetic about attending college. After the botched suicide attempt a "family friend" therapist took only twenty minutes to determine that the seventeen-year-old Kaysen was suffering from "borderline personality disorder," and she was checked into the McLean Psychiatric Hospital (Claymoore, in the film).

It says a lot about how far our understanding of mental illness has progressed that these days such disorders are generally treated with weekly therapy sessions. Kaysen's incarceration lasted from 1967 to 1969. Despite the cultural upheaval rocking America in the 1960s, mental illness was still a dirty little secret. Schizophrenia, manic depression, anorexia, and bulimia weren't yet household words, and family members suffering emotional distress were hidden away. But in Kaysen's stream of consciousness chronicle her troubled teenage self is actually relieved, in a certain sense, to be hidden away. Her struggle becomes to allow herself to heal so that she can rejoin the world; she must not succumb to the temptation to stay cocooned in a place where she really doesn't belong.

Because of its themes it was inevitable that *Girl, Interrupted* would be grouped with certain other films. Industry insiders resorted to the shorthand of comparison to describe the project, referring to it as having a *"One Flew over the Cuckoo's Nest-meets-Stand by Me"* high-concept hook, or as being a *"Snake Pit meets One Flew over the Cuckoo's Nest"* kind of thing. But to Ryder it was simply an obsession; in part because she was somewhat familiar with the territory. Shortly after finishing the film *The House of the Spirits* in 1992 she checked herself into a psychiatric clinic. Just twenty years old at the time, she was having trouble dealing with the stresses arising from too much work, too little sleep, and too little emotional grounding. "I was actually in [the clinic] for five days," says Ryder. "Nineteen was a tough year. For anybody—

whether you're an actress, or cramming for exams, or your parents are driving you crazy, or you're breaking up with your first love. Whatever you're going through, it's a tough year."

Such universal trials were, of course, exacerbated by the grim nature of *The House of the Spirits*, which was released in 1994. "I was playing a political prisoner," recalls Ryder, "and I was doing torture scenes in Portugal. I came back and I was so tired—I've always been a terrible insomniac—and I was so exhausted. I was convinced I was having a nervous breakdown, so I checked myself into a hospital . . . for sleep deprivation—into a clinic, but it was a psychiatric ward. I really got nothing from it. It didn't help me at all. But the thing that I did get is that those places don't really help. You don't go to a place and get a pill that fixes you. They don't give you a sheet of secret answers. You can't pay enough money to have a place fix you. Which is incredibly upsetting when you think that you can. They didn't really offer anything there except for group therapy, which was one hour a day. And that just didn't really do anything for me. I thought, 'I have money and if I pay them enough they're going to have to give me some sort of cure for just feeling broken and confused and just way too sensitive for this insane world.' But it didn't work like that. I left there feeling just the same, pretty much, and just as tired." After all of this, adds Ryder, "the torture scenes in *The House of the Spirits* got cut out, so it was all for nothing!"

Professional ordeals aside, Ryder was also hurting on a more personal level. She had recently broken up with boyfriend Johnny Depp, to whom she was rumored to have been engaged. "The public thinks actors aren't allowed to be depressed," accuses Ryder, "because we're sickeningly well paid, get amazing perks, and live charmed lives. What the public doesn't see is the ugly side of our lives, and that's the stuff that breaks us down. I had broken up with my first real love and there were huge pressures from my career. I needed desperately to take stock of my life, and for that I needed to sleep."

If the clinic fiasco taught Ryder anything it was that she had to help herself. "When I realized I was the only person who could do that for me, I left." She also came to realize that "just because life is weird and messy doesn't mean I have to be miserable. Knowing this has gotten me through a lot of demons and darkness that tried to enter my life." A couple of years later Ryder was presented with the galley proofs of Kaysen's book. The history they contained struck her hard. "Susanna's book spoke to me on a very personal level. It just really captured a mood—that time in your life that is so confusing and so lonely and so oddly funny and weird. It was brutally honest without being self-indulgent. She articulated feelings I hadn't been able to."

Perhaps mingled with Ryder's angst were the aftereffects of a some-times difficult childhood. She was raised near San Francisco, in borderline poverty, by parents who were heavily invested in the coun-terculture experience—the late LSD guru Timothy Leary was little Winona's godfather. The Ryders were also supporters of the arts. "There was an old barn where my mother would play movies," Winona told Chris Norris of *In Style*. "She'd hang a big white sheet and set up the projector. That's where I first saw *East of Eden*—all of Elia Kazan's movies, all John Cassavetes's. She'd show everything, including *Gigi* and *An American in Paris*—those musicals with the amazing, trippy sequences. I think my parents loved those because . . . well, they were smoking a lot of pot."

Ryder began acting when she was twelve. Small movie roles evolved into more prominent ones in such films as *Beetlejuice*, *Heathers*, and *Edward Scissorhands*, the film that brought her together with Johnny Depp. Unlike many child actors, Ryder appeared to make the transi-tion to adult roles with ease, taking on a diverse series of projects—*The Age of Innocence*, *Reality Bites*, and *Alien Resurrection*. She told Norris that she had latched on to *Girl, Interrupted* as a means of "exiting ado-lescence. It's a farewell piece to that time in my life, to all of those roles that I had. I just didn't realize it was going to take seven years to make."

But during that extended interval Ryder had matured and gained a more balanced perspective, one that ultimately allowed the film to become the kind of farewell piece she'd earlier envisioned. But Ryder observes that what her character, Susanna, "learns in the film is that there are no answers, that it's okay not to have answers for everything, that it's okay not to be perfect, that it's okay just to be a human being and be confused, that actually feeling crazy is normal, and that, if you were sitting there feeling that you actually understood the world with war and disease and famine and violence and assassinations and Vietnam, you'd be weird. I'd worry about that person who understood all of those things. So feeling [crazy] is just actually feeling like a human being."

Ryder is usually quite reserved when it comes to discussing personal matters publicly. She made the decision to discuss her own brief stay in the hospital after thinking it over very carefully. She came to the conclusion that by sharing her experience she might help other young women who are trying to cope with loneliness, insecurity, and depression. "I hope I don't come off sounding like just another actor talking about rehab," she says. "I debated whether to talk about it. It happened to me and I'm not ashamed of it, so I felt I should talk about it. These personal things are sent to try us, make us better people, and they certainly have helped to make me a better actress. I wouldn't take away any of my dark moments, but I am happy they're all in my past."

So Ryder was psychologically prepared to portray Susanna Kaysen, but she would need a strong and coherent script to do it. The man Ryder had approached to write the screen adaptation of Kaysen's book, James Mangold, faced a complex task. His raw material was "just kind of these series of vignettes in a mental institution which were neither saying it was a terrible place or a great place but were just kind of events. I felt like someone had to attack the material with vigor and also more loyalty to the feelings, themes, and points of the book." Working in Mangold's favor was the intuitive connection that he believed the audience would feel to the book's subject. "We all wake up and try to figure out why but never are sure. There can be periods of our life that we really can't blame on our ex-girlfriend or mother or anyone, and in fact we just feel shitty. That's interesting. And some people get lost in the spiral of that."

In his effort to translate such phenomena to celluloid, Mangold took a few creative liberties. He expanded on some of the people in Kaysen's book, in particular Lisa, a charming sociopath who revels in troublemaking and button-pushing. Mangold sensed that Lisa manifested a type of freedom that Susanna herself did not possess. "Some of what we think of as crazy is also just speaking the truth all the time," says Mangold, "which, let's face it, we can't do. Part of the rules of life is not saying what you are thinking." To play Lisa, Mangold knew that he would need an actress who had no filters—"Those filters [that] keep you from telling your boss he's an asshole." Whoever she was, she would have to be capable of functioning without social conventions in a convincing way; she would have to be brave enough to fill in the outrageous "coloring book" shapes that Mangold had drawn for her. "All I knew was that the person had to be dangerous, highly verbal, and sexy—a kind of female De Niro."

For a while Mangold despaired of ever finding such an actress. But the problem wasn't that there was a shortage of women who wanted the role. Almost every young, available actress, the well known and the unknown alike, auditioned to play Lisa, but none of them had the indescribable but unmistakable quality that the director was looking for. Until the day Angelina Jolie entered the room. She strode in without a word, plopped herself down on the couch, looked at Mangold, and in that instant he realized he wasn't looking at Angelina Jolie, he was staring into the eyes of Lisa. Interviewed by Anne Bergman of the *Los Angeles Times*, Mangold claimed that auditioning Jolie for the role was one of the "greatest moments" of his life. "It was clear to me that day that I was watching someone who was not acting. There was someone speaking through her, it was a part of herself . . . I not only knew I had Lisa, but that I also had confidence in the movie I had written." Mangold took Jolie through every scene involving Lisa, and when they were done he was "exhausted." But he also knew that Jolie "was going to be Lisa. Not only that, but I actually felt like we had a movie."

Long before that marathon audition Jolie had read Kaysen's book. She told Steve Goldman of *Total Film* about it and went on to add that when she later read the script, "it was that speech at the end that grabbed me, about having buttons and pushing them and not feeling anything. At that point in my life it was like a crying scream that I needed to have . . . I was very happy when I got it. I was screaming." Like Ryder, Jolie had a primal understanding of what Kaysen had attempted to express. "I remember being very upset that I wasn't crazy, that I wasn't a vampire," she told Jessica Holt of *University Wire*. "I wanted to be on stage and think I was someone else."

After winning the role of Lisa, Angelina went to the library and looked up "sociopath." She was directed "to look under serial killers. And you read about them and they're just not aware. They live on impulse so you can't analyze them. You have to throw the books away and say, 'Okay, what do I really feel right now?' and just do it. And sometimes you do things that you're pretty scared of." This is exactly what impressed Mangold about Jolie. "Angie's always exploring," he explains. "She's always digging into finding a reality for herself." The director also points out that plenty of actors can give a good audition; much rarer are those who can deliver the goods over the long haul. Jolie can. "Angie is rebellious, volatile, and really smart," Mangold told Jeffrey Ressner of *Time*. "Playing this role put her in the mode of questioning authority. But if someone delivers the goods like she did, then I'm happy to struggle with the personality." Jolie doesn't deny that she was confrontational during filming. "Acting is not pretending or lying. It's finding a side of yourself that's like the character and ignoring your other sides. And there's a side of me that wonders what's wrong with being completely honest. I get angry when I see people thinking they're better than others. So, yeah, [Lisa's] a lot like me in a certain way."

Playing a sociopath obliged Jolie to curb her natural compassion. In a *beatboxbetty* online interview, she gave this example: "Winona would say that she wasn't feeling well or that she had a tough day because she had a headache . . . and I was like, 'I can't know that as Lisa.' I needed to not feel things. I needed to not feel like we were all together. I needed to feel nothing. I really understand Lisa, but she's more scared than me. She needs to have people accept her right now, or she'll get fuckin' angry and attack them."

Girl, Interrupted, the film, begins in much the same way as *Girl, Interrupted*, the book. It's 1967 and seventeen-year-old Susanna is being sent to a private mental hospital by a psychiatrist who has examined her only briefly. Her fellow patients, all teenagers, are clearly more disturbed than she is. We meet a pathological liar (Clea Duvall), a burn victim who has decided to remain a child (Elizabeth Moss), and a neurotic laxative addict with a daddy complex (Brittany Murphy). Then there is Lisa, who will be the key Susanna requires to journey back to the real world.

Shooting the movie was an incredibly intense, and perhaps even cathartic, experience for Jolie. She told *Playboy*'s Amy Longsdorf, "I have scenes where I'm actually strapped to a bed, which, for me, raises a lot of interesting issues. I mean, there is something strange and kinky to all that stuff. The movie takes place in the sixties, and just learning what they did to people back then is horrifying. There's one girl in there because she's gay. I wish they'd focused more on that character. It's so sad to think that someone was given shock treatments just because they're unsure of their sexuality." Increasing the intensity of the experience for Jolie was the fact that this time she didn't feel as comfortable with her castmates as she had in the past. "I don't generally get along with women," she confessed to Deanna Kizis of *Harper's Bazaar*, apparently forgetting the sorority-style camaraderie she had enjoyed while making *Foxfire*. "I don't gossip, and I'm not really sensitive, so this can hurt people's feelings." Much of this stemmed from the perception that Jolie was snubbing one particular young actress; and the drama that ensued annoyed Jolie. "I work with guys a lot of times and that never happens, you know? If I come on set and my character has a particularly heavy scene that day, no guy has ever come up to me, you know, like, 'You were really rude to me yesterday.' But that happens sometimes with girls."

If Brittany Murphy, who played Daisy, was the offended party, then she hid it well in press interviews. She joked with reporters that she didn't have to do much research to play a mental patient because, "You have to be a little crazy to be an actor. You spend your life pretending to be other people. That's not exactly normal. Acting is not the most stable profession in the world." Murphy then claimed that neither Ryder nor Jolie had come up for air very often. "It was rare to see either of them out of character for the entire twelve-week shoot. Angelina's character, Lisa, really hated Daisy, so she shunned me. One day she began talking to me and then stopped cold. She stared hard at me, and Angelina was replaced by Lisa, and she walked away. She was always teasing me about the wig I had to wear for Daisy. At the end of the shoot she gave me a backpack with a dog that had exactly the same hairstyle. I think it was her way of telling me there were no hard feelings. It was just part of her acting process." As for Ryder, Murphy continued, she "never actually acknowledged the other actors on a day-to-day basis. She started being Susanna the moment she arrived on the set for makeup. It's not the way I'm used to working, but I think it really worked for this movie because it is so intense."

Mangold was unfazed by such behavior. To him, blurring the lines between reality and fiction is what acting is all about. "In order to play any character in a movie," Mangold insists, "you're not doing what I do, which is to try and take in the whole picture. Angelina is playing Lisa as if it's Lisa's picture, always Lisa's picture, completely Lisa's movie, just about Lisa. And if she's doing something mean to some-body—or something you might think is mean to somebody—she ain't playin' it like she's doing something mean to somebody. She's not going, 'Ahh, this is the scene where I'm a bitch.' She's thinking of the scene like, 'I'm trying to do an intervention. I'm trying to get through to this person who's fuckin' getting lost.' That's how she sees it. So if ultimately, somehow, when it's rendered on the screen, some segment of the audi-ence thinks or perceives it as you've crossed the line, or you were a little shitty to this person . . . it's part of why she's so damn good."

Jolie now admits that she might not have been the most pleasant person to hang out with during filming. Of Ryder, she says, "I know our characters were very different, and I think in many ways it was scarier for her to play that role. I took on a personality so full of force, and she took on a personality that was scared, so the two of us together . . . I'm sure I was not lovely in the morning to her, you know. But I was very proud of her. I was very proud of how much this affected her, how hard she worked. I'm a little crazy, probably, in comparison. I'm a little out of my mind." Imagining for twelve weeks straight that you're someone dangling over the edge of an abyss does take a toll. "It was so unsettling it was settling," Angelina recalls. "I didn't try to put a bunch of things on [Lisa] to make her crazy, I just thought of it as living on impulse. And then I became very grounded with it and went through the movie not feeling very much and having fun. It's really hard to talk about because I *was* her, so it's hard to kind of look at it from the outside. I know where Lisa is coming from. I can scare people off pretty easily, and I know how to push people's buttons. Like Lisa, I feel that people aren't really honest with me and that makes me pull away. I have this quote from Tennessee Williams tattooed on my upper arm. It says, 'A prayer for the wild at heart kept in cages.' That's Lisa. That's me."

Angelina credits Mangold with keeping her from spiraling way out of control while she was Lisa. "He corralled me, I guess. He encour-aged certain things; he kept me focused so I didn't go all over the place. I mean, I did, but I didn't go really all over the place. I think with Winona, he wanted her to get a little off track. But there's some

times I need to shut my head off and just make the choice and just do it and be simpler."

Probably more than anything else it was the prerelease buzz about Jolie's performance in *Girl, Interrupted* that boasted the film's notoriety. Its release was eagerly anticipated, and those responsible for its creation began to wonder how audiences would react to its harrowing subject matter. Teen comedies were a safe bet; teen dramas were something else entirely. "this is one of those movies that lives and dies on being good," said Michael Costigan, senior VP of production at Columbia, the studio behind *Girl, Interrupted*. Then a confident Costigan added, "And considering the director and the cast we're lining up, I think it's going to be amazing." In fact, Columbia was so convinced that Jolie's performance was award-worthy that it arranged for the film to have a one-week December release so that it would qualify for 1999 Academy Award consideration.

The studio's hunch was good. The critics were almost blown away by Jolie, favoring her with the best reviews of her already well-reviewed career. Most liked the movie, too. *Entertainment Weekly*'s Owen Gleiberman gave the film an A-minus and declared, "*Girl, Interrupted* is shrewd, tough, and lively—a junior-league *One Flew Over the Cuckoo's Nest* that never makes the mistake of portraying its protago- nist as a victim-naif. She's more like the original poster child for Prozac Nation: a girl who'd rather interrupt her own life, even if it means going a little cuckoo, than grow up. Most of the patients are harmless, but Lisa (Angelina Jolie), a heartless, charismatic sociopath, delights in her destructive power. Jolie brings the kind of combustible sexuality to the screen that our movies, in the age of Meg Ryan, have been missing for too long."

Newsday's Gene Seymour told his readers that "Jolie livens things up, even—or especially—when Lisa's being very bad. Alone among the cast, she seems to have emerged from a time warp straight from the 1960s, oozing the sexy, scary recklessness of that era. Ryder is well cast and keeps things anchored. Even at her best, she never makes you forget her star persona the way Jolie does." And Chris Vognar of the *Dallas Morning News* called Jolie "a dangerous live wire here. Eyes blaring, lips pouting, she gives a stunning portrayal of living perilously in the moment at the expense of friends and bystanders. The part should finally cement Ms. Jolie's status as one of the most convincing young actresses around, one of the few who can disappear without a trace into a tough role."

Geoff Pevere of the *Toronto Star* was not entranced with the film, but Jolie's performance had him waxing eloquent: "While *Girl, Interrupted* demonstrates the same facility for layered performance and character-centered drama, the film suffers because its main character doesn't suffer enough. Which is why Jolie, bringing to her performance as nuthouse-lifer Lisa something of the glassy-eyed suicide-chic she demonstrated in the T.V.-biopic *Gia*, wipes the hospital floors with Ryder whenever Lisa's around."

Accolades were heaped upon Angelina, but when she alluded to her latest triumph it almost seemed as though she feared losing the angst and turmoil that had brought her to it. Emotional pain was her muse. "I'm very pleased where my career is at, but I have so many other sides of myself," she said to Brent Simon of *Entertainment Today*. "There are so many parts of your life that are not perfect . . . or not even good, so it's funny when people say, 'This must be just such a great time for you,' and I'm thinking, 'This is probably the worst time of my life in many ways!' I try not to think about this stuff." Perfection may have seemed elusive, not to mention peace of mind, but none of this appeared to affect the astonishing momentum of Jolie's career. She was bound for greater and greater success.

There are certain performances that almost everyone agrees are awesome. In 1999 moviegoers and critics alike were blown away by Hilary Swank in *Boys Don't Cry* and Angelina Jolie in *Girl, Interrupted*. Both were tour de force performances, and on the strength of them the two actresses swept up just about every award except the Miss America crown. For the third time in her brief career Jolie won a Golden Globe, this time in the Best Supporting Actress in a Film Drama category (accepting the honor, she dragged her brother onstage with her as the puzzled audience looked on). So when the 1999 Academy Awards were announced in February 2000 it was no surprise that Jolie's name was on the list.

The day the Oscar nominations were made public was the most momentous of Jolie's career to date, but the young nominee was nowhere to be found in Hollywood. Instead of basking in the glorious blaze of attention that followed the announcement, Jolie was off in Mexico filming *Dancing in the Dark*. Michael Cristofer, who had guided Jolie through her *Gia* paces, was her director, and Antonio Banderas was her handsome leading man (later Jolie had to squelch rumors arising from reports that Melanie Griffith, Banderas's wife, had found the film's steamy sex scenes all too believable). In this latest screen adaptation of Cornell Woolrich's suspense novel *Waltz into Darkness*, Jolie played a deceptive seductress who marries a wealthy tycoon in turn-of-the-century New Orleans. But when entertainment reporters clamoring for her response to the Oscar nomination finally reached her by phone, Jolie slipped out of character long enough to say, "All the women in my category are so cool. I just feel so lucky today."

As Oscar night approached, Jolie's anxiety level mounted. She was still in Mexico shooting *Dancing in the Dark*, but she would be permitted to return to Los Angeles for the awards ceremony. "I get nervous and don't eat as much, even though I remind myself," she admitted in an interview published in Australia's *Sunday Mail*. "I'm trying to put weight on. I'm hoping to get on a program soon." She also said that her dad had been trying to force feed her. When the big day, March 26th, finally dawned, Jolie was clearly relieved that she would soon be out of the pressure cooker. She arrived at the ceremony with Brother James, clinging to him as though he alone could hold her upright as she ran the red-carpet gauntlet to the door of L.A.'s Shrine Auditorium. Flash-bulbs popped; people were calling "Angelina!"; and Jolie became so consumed by this sideshow that she lingered a little too long and got locked out of the auditorium. The Best Supporting Actress Oscar is often among the first to be doled out during the awards ceremony, so Jolie was in a panic. She pleaded with security to let her in, thinking of how disappointed her mother would be if her daughter missed her big moment. Finally, James Coburn, the previous year's Best Supporting Actor and the presenter of Jolie's category, managed to get her through the door. And not a moment too soon. A little while later the envelope was unsealed and Angelina Jolie was proclaimed the winner. About the only person in attendance who appeared surprised was Angelina herself, and she seemed dumbstruck. She leaned over and gave her brother, who had tears streaming down his face, a rather long kiss before making her way to the podium. "I'm surprised nobody's ever fainted up here," she began, with a quiver in her voice. "I'm—I'm in shock. And I'm so in love with my brother right now. He just held me and said he loved me. And I know he's so happy for me. And thank you for that. And thank you to Columbia. Winona, you're amazing, and thank you for supporting all of us through this. And all the girls in this film are amazing." Angelina rushed on, thanking her family, "for loving me . . . my mom, who is the most brave, beautiful woman I've ever known. And my dad. You're a great actor, but you're a better father. And Jamie, you're just— I have nothing without you. You are the strongest, most amazing man I've ever known, and I love you . . ." Backstage Jolie gripped her award, bedazzled. "I really didn't expect this," she repeated. "Dad has an Oscar. It's something you strive for all your life, to do something that's acknowledged like this."

Surrounded by reporters that night Jolie fielded a range of questions. When asked about the woman on whom the character of Lisa was based, she replied, "She hasn't decided to be in very much contact with me. I'm thinking she probably won't until all of this blows over with all of you. She's living her life. At the end of the book she had a child, a boy so that child is probably around my age now. And I think she's in New York, but I would guess she's gone through a lot, and she's kind of maybe just now settling." Another journalist wanted to know whether Jolie was disappointed that the Shrine Auditorium had no swimming pool for her to jump into. Jolie smiled devilishly and answered, "I mentioned to somebody something about a roof at the Shrine, but I'm not sure I can get on it in this dress. I'm sure I'm going to do something. Yeah—I'm going to have to. I'm too happy. I'm excited, you know. Some weird things happen when I get excited."

In a more serious mood, Angelina tried to articulate the thoughts that had rushed through her head when she heard her name announced. "I really didn't expect it. I just hid in my brother's arms, and I think in both of our minds we both were just like, 'Oh, my!' We grew up in this business, and dad has an Oscar, and it's like the big thing you try to attain as an actor, to do a performance that's really acknowledged and means something. And so, you know, it's always been a big deal to us, this show. We've always watched it, so we both were sitting [there and] going, 'Do you believe we're here and they let us in?'"

Brotherly love...

When questioned about her close relationship to her brother, Jolie looked thoughtful. "Oh, God, well, I don't know if it's divorced families or what it is, but he and I were each other's everything, always, and we've been best friends. Maybe it's just [being] my brother, but he's always been my strongest support, and he's the funniest person I know. He's the sweetest human being I know. He's a good person, and he's just given me so much love and taken care of me, and you know, it makes life great. He's my friend." Referring to James's reaction when her name was called, Jolie said, "I don't think he could really move. I think he stayed in his seat. He was very emotional."

Surprisingly, Jolie confessed that she had never held an Oscar in her hands until this very night, when she'd won her own. "My dad's mother had his in a goldfish bowl, or something, on the mantelpiece in New York. It was way up in something. And I've never held it. Growing up with it, you figure it's the strange thing in grandma's house, but you know, I don't remember much about it." She also recalled attending the Oscars with her father when she was very young and seeing "some empty seats. And I think you had cartoon characters painted in. And I remember being a little girl and realizing they weren't actually there and being really upset."

Coming back to the role that had just won her a statuette of her own, Jolie described how she felt when she was first confronted with the script of *Girl, Interrupted*. "Generally when I read a script and I'm scared to play the role, I know it's the right one. And I was scared to death of Gia because I thought it was just going to expose too much to myself about myself, and I didn't think I could do it, and I thought it was important to do it right. And when I read this, she made me cry, Lisa. Different things I read—it hurt me. It was important to me, and I didn't even want to go over the lines because I was deeply affected by her. And then I decided that somebody had to speak, you know. I wanted her to have a voice really strongly, so I thought maybe I wanted more than anybody for her to be heard, so maybe it should be me. But it's always hard to say I'm the right person for something. But I wanted this part."

As the night wore on, Jolie's thoughts turned more and more towards her family. She told reporters that earlier in the day, "both of my parents came over to the hotel when I was getting ready. They both surprised

Angelina wins at the 72nd Academy Awards

me and brought gifts." Her mother, Marcheline, brought everyone a corsage, and Voight brought Marcheline a gift, as well; he wanted to thank her for helping to guide their daughter's career. Then Angelina told a story about being with her mother a few days before. "And I said, 'Mom, you need a new car.' She said, 'But you went on all of your auditions in this car. You lost a hundred jobs in this car.' And she got emotional and said, 'Can you believe you're going to the Oscars?' You know, that's my mom. My dad came in and said he was proud of me and that I was a good actress. To hear that from your father, for him to think I'm a good actress, is kind of a big deal to me, so that was all I needed, and he loved me, and that's all that mattered."

After that unforgettable night was over Jolie told *Talk* magazine that she'd phoned Marcheline from backstage, and "she was having a fucking heart attack. My father had called her—he'd been at Spago waiting for me—and apparently the two of them were on the phone crying, which is wonderful. When they saw me say to my brother, 'I love you,' they saw how much their two children love each other and how we're going to be okay always because we have each other. So they were, like, out of their minds. And three hours later I was on Air Mexicana back to shoot *Dancing in the Dark*." And Jeannie Williams of *USA Today* later caught up with James Haven, who admitted to her, "I've never had the emotions kick in as much as tonight. I just started shaking. I wanted to stand up and give her a big hug, but I couldn't get out of my chair. Then she starts talking about me, and I start crying again."

Throughout her life Angelina professed her love for James freely and effusively; it was entirely in keeping with her nature that she would experience love of any kind with the same intensity she experienced general life. Plus, James was her big brother—they'd grown up together and he'd helped and encouraged her in her acting. Of course, Angelina was acutely aware that her career had rocketed past James's, and she wanted to share the fun by bringing him along for the ride and by supporting him as he worked to make his own mark on the profession—which is why Haven has had small roles in many of Jolie's films (he's the one who looks like Angelina). But on Oscar night, with none of this context in evidence, the Shrine Auditorium audience and the millions of people watching on television just saw a very excited young actress ardently declaring her love for her brother. Quite a few eyebrows were raised, and in the weeks and months that followed speculation swirled that Angelina and James had an incestuous relationship.

"It's a really weird thing," Haven said to Elizabeth Snead of *USA Today*. "I laughed at first, then I got angry about it. Now that I have had time to think, I think it's just that people are not used to this, so they automatically think negatively. But everyone who has jumped to this very sick thought is going to have egg on their face. They are writing all these stories that will be there forever, and they will realize in time that it is just a very close relationship and it has nothing to do with what they are implying." Then Haven's mischievous sense of humor—so like his sister's—kicked in. He told Snead that he was thinking of getting his first tattoo, and it would read "Angelina." Jolie just shrugged off the rumors. "He's my best friend," she said to Snead. Then came the typical Jolie follow-up: "The thing is, if I *were* sleeping with my brother, I would tell people I was. People know that about me."

Soon enough, Haven's prediction came true, and those journalists who'd given credence to the incest rumors had egg on their faces. By the time she won her Academy Award Jolie was already involved in a passionate secret affair with the man she'd been waiting for all her life. And it wouldn't be long before their secret was out.

ELEVEN

LOVE AND PEACE

Jolie had been one very popular covergirl before winning her Oscar. Once the award was on her mantelpiece virtually every magazine wanted to display her face. She obliged a lot of them but she wasn't always convinced that it was such a good idea. "I'll be jumping around and feeling sexy," she explained in *Maxim*. "Then the pictures come out, and I'll be in a bustier top, sucking on a shoe, and my friends will go, 'What did you do that for?'

All of the attention, the interviews, the photo shoots, were sapping her energies; plus, she still hadn't fully recovered from making *Girl, Interrupted*. She knew she needed a break. "When I finished *Girl, Interrupted* I wasn't going to work for a while," Jolie says. "During the shoot I wasn't getting what I needed to nourish me because I was kind of doing cartwheels for everybody. At the end of the day I was exhausted because I had been out on a limb and I didn't have anybody there. And then that hit me at the end of the shoot." So it was decided. She's take time off.

Why then, did she agree to do *Gone in 60 Seconds*, the Nicolas Cage film, in which the actor plays a master car thief forced to pull off one more heist to save his brother? Because, Angelina says, "I was not going to hardly work. I had a very short schedule. It was not going to be emotional in any way. It *was* taking time off. I needed to be silly. I needed to be around Nic [Cage] and those guys, who are really nice people, and just have a really silly time with them." In a *beatboxbetty* online interview, she added, "Nic's amazing. He's a really great team leader and he supports all of the other actors. He lets them do their thing. He seems very serious but he's also completely nuts and free. He's a great guy and he deserves everything that's happening for him."

Reflecting on the fact that a lot of moviegoers would wonder why she followed up her Oscar-winning role in a drama with a part in an action flick, Jolie says, "There are so many people who are saying, 'You're doing this B movie?' It's like they expect more from you and that's terrible. I just wanted to play. And I wanted to be around a lot of men. I'd been around women in a mental institution for way too long." In any case, she explains, "If I'm not working I'm not focused. It's where I feel useful . . . I'm not good at being me."

To Steve Goldman of *Total Film* she also maintained that she'd been attracted to the role of Sarah in *Gone in 60 Seconds* because she was "just a clean, blue-collar girl under a car with a bunch of guys. Thank God. For me it was like this little part in this light film. And then suddenly it's like, 'This is a Jerry Bruckheimer Film.' It's certainly bigger than any of my work." It was also a role that Bruckheimer, the producer of such big-budget extravaganzas as *Top Gun*, had written specifically for her. "Angelina is definitely in the top echelon of actresses," he told Elizabeth Snead of *USA Today*. "She is on everyone's A list. She does so much with just a look. Through her eyes, you can see into her soul, see both her joy and her pain. You want to watch her on screen, and that is what makes a movie star. Maybe it's genetic." How could Angelina resist that vote of confidence?

But in the end, *Gone in 60 Seconds*, a hundred-million-dollar remake of H.B. Halicki's 1974 cult classic, was little more than summer popcorn fare—lots of cars and crashes. Filming was half over before Jolie even had to show up for work. When she did, she was showing off a brand new hairstyle. She'd thought about the character of Sarah "Sway" Rayland and decided that long blonde dreadlocks would work. "I knew she was going to be the only girl amongst the guys, and she had to be kind of tough," she explained to Angela Dawson of *Newsday*. "But I thought it was very important not to lose the sense that she is very much a woman. So I wanted her to have long hair and look like one of those car magazine girls as opposed to the obvious tomboy/ greaser type. But I also thought she had to be the kind of girl who wouldn't bother doing anything with her hair—washing it or putting it back or anything. So dreads made sense."

While Jolie considered the project to be a kind of working vacation, she seized the opportunity to bone up on a subject that she hadn't known much about before. To Cindy Pearlman of Australia's *Daily Telegraph*, she remarked, "Frankly I wanted to learn about cars. I do know how to steal a car now, although maybe I shouldn't let that out there. We actually had a real thief on the set, escorted by his prison guard. I didn't know who they were the first time. I thought they were two prop guys and then I got the skinny. I asked the thief a million questions and this guy could rip apart an entire car and tell you every single part of it."

As it turned out, *Gone in 60 Seconds* was aptly titled. That's about how long it lasted in movie theaters. Critics barely wasted any ink on it, and most of the reviews that did appear took a similar tone to Dave Thompson's in *Salon*: "*Gone in 60 Seconds* isn't just rubbish, it's Nicolas Cage and PG-13 rubbish . . . Unless he's very careful, the only audience he has will be boys young enough to mistake monotony for deep acting." Yet Jolie, predictably, scored again. Continued Thompson, "Angelina Jolie is another matter. She's the kind of treasure that no one has the least idea how to handle . . . She has in her own way what very few American women have had—Louise Brooks, Jean Harlow, Tuesday Weld, Marilyn Monroe—and what they were seldom allowed to deliver."

Gone in 60 Seconds was released in June 2000. By that time Jolie's feelings for Billy Bob Thornton burgeoned. Angelina Jolie was in love. Not the sweetness-and-light, hearts-and-flowers kind, but the lose-your-mind, get-scared-of-losing-control kind. Crazy love. Still, back in January 2000 Jolie was speaking like someone resigned to being alone. Since her divorce she'd dated here and there, but she felt emotionally isolated. She insisted to Louis Hobson of the *Edmonton Sun*, "I'm very happy to be on my own. I have a lot of really great male friends so I don't feel I need intimacy. I love hanging out with my male friends. It's cool with them to have me around because we've gotten past that fuzzy sexual thing that intimidates men unless it's addressed." In other interviews,

Jolie would take responsibility for her single state, acknowledging that because she worked so much she had made herself unavailable for a serious relationship. "It's not fair to the other person that I'm so busy with my career and that I'm often distant even when I am with someone."

While filming *Gone in 60 Seconds*, Jolie's divorce was finalized, and her long-dead marriage was officially over. Her relationship with Miller may have been ancient history, but its demise on paper still pained Angelina. That, along with the residual effects of her *Girl, Interrupted* experience and the illness of a close friend, conspired to undermine her physical well-being. People began noticing that Jolie was looking pretty ragged, and speculation heated up. "I had stress," Jolie told Deanna Kizis of *Jane*. "I didn't look well, my face broke out, I showed up on the set, and they said, 'You go home.' Somehow it made a bunch of people very upset with me because they didn't know whatever was going on. I didn't feel like explaining somebody's private business, but you suddenly think, god, here I am looking really skinny, and I can't eat . . . I just went through an emotional time. But when you do that in this business, you realize the ugliness of what the worst in their eyes would be, that people are thinking that you're sick. If in the future I ever was, this is how little people would help me." Jolie then insisted that everyone on *Gone in 60 Seconds* was great to her, but the experience still made her "yearn for a normal life."

From portraying herself as the happy single in interview situations, Jolie had shifted her tone and was now musing about settling down and having children. Still just in her mid-twenties, she wanted to make a family. She admitted that while she was wide open to adoption, people had cautioned her against it, saying that her wild youthful antics and her penchant for appearing on magazine covers scantily clad would damage her chances of being approved as an adoptive parent. The idea that she would be rejected for experiencing personal and creative growing pains infuriated Jolie; it was just further evidence of society's twisted values. But as her vision of domesticity developed, Jolie turned away from talk of adoption and started to speak to her interviewers about her ideal mate. She insisted on passion: "It should be a combination of thinking, 'I love you but I just want to rip that apart and eat you.' I just haven't found that person to break through with. But I've just gotten signs."

Then suddenly all the signs were flashing. For nearly a year, Jolie had been quietly seeing Thornton, who was involved with actress Laura Dern. Then passion became true love and the Jolie-Thornton romance hit the media. Dern was devastated. *Us Weekly* noted that in the May issue of *Men's Journal* Billy Bob had spoken glowingly of Dern, saying, "I'm now happily involved with someone who's my best friend. We have a dog and a yard and I have my kids [two sons and a daughter from previous unions] part of the time." But in April stories had begun circulating that Thornton's fidelity was suspect, and, according to J.D. Heyman of *Us*, Dern's mother, actress Diane Ladd, had angrily accused him of being, "Dr. Jekyll and Mr. Hyde. Billy Bob told me he wants my daughter to be his wife, and I know they've talked about having kids. I don't know how to make sense out of it."

As with all such stories, it's difficult to separate the fact from the fiction because once it becomes public everyone puts their own spin on things to avoid looking bad. It is certain, though, that Billy Bob and Angelina met during the spring of 1998 while filming *Pushing Tin*. Jolie even admitted in a *Talk* magazine interview that she was interested in Thornton from the very first moment they met. "When I first met him I was in shock. We were friends for so long, but I was shocked at the way I reacted to this other person. I just went on with my life, but I never really forgot . . . I never enjoyed anybody just sitting and talking." However, she also stated that their romance hadn't begun in earnest until some time later. "We were both living our lives. I didn't know if anything would ever be possible, you know? I honestly never expected. I liked him too much to think he should ever be near somebody like me. I just didn't think much of myself. And I realize that says a lot. I wanted to be better as a person. So I don't know what it was. It was just really caring more about somebody, really wanting them to live their life and do the things they do." But, she added, "recently I've been able to start spending time with that person, and nothing else matters."

It's clear, as well, that by March 2000 the relationship had turned romantic. Not only was Angelina spotted with a new tattoo that read "Billy Bob," but she was also flying into Los Angeles from the Mexican location of *Dancing in the Dark* every chance she got. She had spent some time with Thornton after the Oscar ceremony, before her 4:00 A.M.

flight back to Mexico. Asked in the *beatboxbetty* online interview how she'd managed to keep her volatile secret, Jolie answered simply, "I don't think anybody was looking for it!" Certainly not Laura Dern, who had been involved with Thornton ever since the actor had split from his fourth wife, Pietra Dawn, shortly after the 1997 Academy Awards ceremony, during which he received an Oscar for his *Sling Blade* screenplay.

The divorce proceedings between Thornton and Dawn were bitter; she charged that he was physically abusive and described him as a manic depressive who turned violent when he stopped taking his lithium. (Billy Bob has been open about overcoming his past alcohol abuse and eating disorders.) As the proceedings went on, the accusations flew fast and thick. Each claimed the other had made death threats, and the presiding judge issued restraining orders against both.

This was the kind of baggage Thornton came to Jolie with, and she appeared to accept it with grace. But for all the happiness Jolie would later express about her relationship with Thornton, she has never fully explained the one disturbing press report that emerged in May 2000. According to Australia's *Sunday Mail*, a short time before eloping with Thornton, Jolie checked herself into the Neuropsychiatric Institute at UCLA Medical Center. Sources at the hospital confirmed that Jolie was admitted for three days after Thornton gave her an ultimatum: marry him or he'd go back to Dern. "She said she was afraid she would hurt herself," said a hospital insider. "She was very angry and thought she might kill herself if she wasn't treated." A spokesperson for the actress confirmed that Jolie had indeed checked into the hospital—to be treated for that all-purpose malady Hollywood publicists term "exhaustion." But the fact that within twenty-four hours of leaving the hospital Jolie was a new bride lends the *Sunday Mail* report some credence, especially since Angelina was still insisting publicly that she thought she wouldn't make a good wife to anyone. She told Stephanie Mansfield of *USA Weekend*, "I still don't know if I'm the best person to be in his life, to live side by side. I love him that much. I didn't want him as much as I wanted him to have a good life."

Although some reporters had jumped the gun and announced that Thornton and Jolie had gotten married in April, the couple actually got hitched on May 5th. They recited their vows in Las Vegas at the

Little Church of the West, a chapel on the Vegas Strip that has been the site of several celebrity weddings. In 1991, Cindy Crawford and Richard Gere exchanged vows there; among the other big names to hold their nuptials at the chapel are Judy Garland, Zsa Zsa Gabor, and Oasis's Noel Gallagher.

According to various news reports, Thornton and Jolie arrived at the Little Church of the West in the midafternoon. They both wore jeans, and they were accompanied by Billy Bob's best friend, Harve Cook, who would serve as best man. Nobody from Jolie's family was present. Their wedding package cost two hundred dollars—that included the ceremony (performed by the Reverend James Hamilton), photos, flowers (a rose and carnation bouquet), and music ("Unchained Melody" by the Righteous Brothers). James Haven revealed to J.D. Heyman of *Us Weekly* that his sister had called to tell him the news of her marriage after the wedding was over. He'd never even been introduced to the groom. "I asked her if she was happy," Haven recalls. "She said, 'Yes, this is it.'" Haven added that Thornton had later left him a message, saying, "Brother, I can't wait to meet you." Wanting only the best for Angelina, James seemed willing to suspend his doubts about the durability of quickie Hollywood marriages and maintained, "Marriage is special. I believe it's forever. Billy Bob's been married a lot, and my sister has been married once. So I want to say, 'Prove me right, guys. Make the happiness stay.'"

John Voight had met Billy Bob Thornton before. They'd worked on the 1997 film *U-Turn* together. When he'd been asked to comment on his daughter's rumored romance with Thornton, Voight had told the *Daily Telegraph*, "The media always knows more than a father. I've met Billy Bob, but never as someone who was seeing my daughter." After her marriage, Jolie insisted to Elizabeth Snead that her father approved of her choice, despite the fact that he seemed reserved about the whole thing. "My dad likes [Billy Bob]. I wasn't sure how it would work out; I mean, they are fellow actors. But my dad loves me so much, and he's never seen me so happy, so of course he likes him." And even if Voight didn't, Jolie was probably too enraptured to notice.

Thornton was pretty enraptured himself. "In terms of relationships," he said to Liz Braun of the *Ottawa Sun*, "this may be the first time in my life that I haven't failed. Angelina is everything to me as a human being, as an artist, and as a partner. I was looking at her sleep and I had to restrain myself from literally squeezing her to death. Sex for us is almost too much." The two arrived at the premiere of *Gone in 60 Seconds* arm in arm. They were unable to keep their hands off one another.

Love, Angelina asserted, was changing her. It was bringing out character traits she never knew she possessed. "I've never known what it was to be jealous, obsessive," she said to Mansfield. "Wanting to talk constantly. Now I don't like being by myself. When I was friends with this person, I was worried if I was good enough—never if *he* was good enough. I used to feel that my work was why I was alive. I wasn't born to love another person. Now I feel there is something more special. I used to not be afraid to die. Now I'm so happy living. I don't want to miss a moment."

Jolie also talked about feeling more grounded since becoming involved with Thornton. She confessed during press interviews that, "Suddenly, overnight, I'm more content, more alive, and my life has taken on meaning. He is my strength, and he makes me so proud of myself and reminds me that everything is okay. Now, being centered, calm, and safe, I feel more alive than ever and really free. He is the most amazing person I have ever met in my life. He is really a free spirit, bold, really strong and passionate and wild and all those things. But he is also a very kind person, a really good friend." And to *Talk* magazine, she described her new husband as "the sexiest fucking creature that ever lived."

Well aware that her hasty marriage would evoke skepticism in many quarters, Jolie remarked in her *beatboxbetty* online interview, "You know you always expect a certain amount of criticism and we've had that, too, but we are very much in love and we are going to share our lives with people. We don't mind. And we hope people are rooting for us rather than being against us." But what did it matter in the end? Angelina was convinced that she'd mated for life. "I know it will be forever," she declared to David Germain in the *Dallas Morning News*. As far as Billy Bob's marital track record went, Angelina would only defend it: "If I didn't meet him until I was older, during those years I probably would have been married four times, too. This is different. I know we've found each other now."

Playing some foosball with Billy Bob

So marriage had transformed her personal life. But it also put her professional life into a new perspective. As a single woman Jolie had found that her work helped fill the void created by her loneliness. Now, as a married woman, she wanted to work less—home was suddenly a place she wanted to be. The idea of working with her husband had also entered her mind. But first Angelina had one last movie commitment to fulfill: a potential blockbuster called *Tomb Raider*, which was to be shot in London. If ever there was a film role that could both stretch Jolie's screen persona in new directions and catapult her into the superstar stratosphere it was that of Lara Croft, *Tomb Raider*'s shapely heroine. In this age of digital convergence, Croft is a custom-built star—a video-game character who is revered by the techno masses as if she were flesh and blood.

Lara Croft was conceived as a kind of female Indiana Jones, and her mission was to anchor the *Tomb Raider* video-game series. She was also intended to be, in somewhat indelicate terms, every schoolboy's wet dream. This glowing video image boasts a 34D-24-35 figure and an impossibly lean and toned five-foot-nine-inch frame; she has a lustrous mane of dark hair. Her physical appeal is matched only by her toughness, which has been honed by her adventures as an archeologist with a mission. She can seduce an enemy with a look or shoot him down before he knows what's happening. She's a disinherited British blueblood who must turn to such activities as tomb raiding and writing travel books (with names like *A Tyrannosaurus Is Jawing at My Head*) to pay for the upkeep on her mansion in Surrey, which is filled with the artifacts she has acquired on her travels. On the grounds of the estate, Lara has constructed an assault course for training purposes.

When she made her debut in the 1996 action game *Tomb Raider*, Lara Croft became an overnight worldwide phenomenon. She is, arguably, the first virtual celebrity. She has appeared on over two hundred magazine covers around the world; she was profiled in the December 1999 edition of *Time* magazine, and she's also appeared in *Newsweek*, *Rolling Stone*, and *Entertainment Weekly*'s *It* issue, which spotlights the hundred most creative people in entertainment. The *London Times* recently devoted a special sixteen-page supplement to her, and *Time Digital* included her on its list of the fifty members of America's cyber-elite, a list that included Bill Gates, Steve Jobs, and George Lucas.

Details magazine even named this artificial creation one of the "Sexiest Women of the Year."

Evidence of her staggering success is everywhere. Lara Croft has challenged the supremacy of the supermodels, appearing in television advertising campaigns in North America, Europe, and Asia. She is the subject of more than a thousand Internet fan sites—each created independently of Eidos, the company that manufactures the *Tomb Raider* games. Her image has been merchandised in the form of action figures, comic books, and a clothing line. Lara's success has even inspired the world-famous Elite modeling agency to open an entire division devoted to developing virtual models; others are now following Elite's lead.

What's particularly remarkable about Lara Croft is that a few short years ago female action figures were considered a hard sell. The conventional wisdom was that game players only wanted good guys and bad guys—the operative word being *guys*—along with various monsters and aliens. No women need apply. Eidos Interactive changed all that with Lara Croft. Eidos executive Gary Keith illuminates the company's thinking: "The core audience—males in the thirteen-to-thirty-five age bracket—loves to see this beautiful, buxom woman running around. They prefer this eye candy to game heroes who are rendered into Arnold Schwarzeneggers." By accident Eidos discovered that Lara Croft also had crossover appeal. Says Keith, "Women like Lara Croft because they perceive her as a role model: she's not only adventurous but very well educated." Buxom and brainy—the potent combination has made *Tomb Raider* one of the most successful video and PC games of all time.

Yet another key to *Tomb Raider*'s success is, without a doubt, its manufacturer's attention to plot detail. Four titles in the series—*Tomb Raider, Tomb Raider II: Dagger of Xian, Tomb Raider III: Adventures of Lara Croft,* and *Tomb Raider: The Last Revelation*—have sold over twenty-one-million units, with each heading the PlayStation and PC-game bestseller lists. In all, *Tomb Raider* game sales and related-merchandise sales have generated five hundred million dollars for Eidos Interactive. It's little wonder that Paramount Studios went after the film rights: the ready-made audience for a *Tomb Raider* film would be enormous, and the game series is a bountiful source of material for any screenwriter assigned to the project. Coproducer Lloyd Levin, of course, agrees, describing *Tomb Raider* and Lara Croft as properties that are "well suited for film adaptation. Not only because of the game's thematic and visual richness, but also because it's so strongly character- and story-oriented." After securing those rights, Paramount pulled out all the stops, approving a budget for the film in excess of one hundred million dollars.

As Jolie prepares to play a video icon, she's feeling the pressure. "Actually, I'm frightened about it," she told Jack Stenze of *Entertainment Weekly*. "Do I look like an action hero to you?" Sounding as though she's on the road to becoming one, however, she added, "There's gonna be a lot of kick-ass action, for sure." Others involved in the project are confident that when the time comes Jolie will kick ass just as hard as Lara Croft. Paul Baldwin, VP of marketing for Eidos comments, "We signed the deal for the film back in 1997, and figured they'd cast some unknown in the part. Getting someone like Angelina Jolie was beyond our wildest dreams. Having an actor of her caliber is wonderful for the film, and she's got both the looks and the attitude for the part."

Tomb Raider is set to break box-office records when it hits movie screens in the summer of 2001, and in the meantime Jolie has been circling her character, trying to get a fix on her. Her portrayal of Lara, she promises, will not be "campy and stupid. We're making her a little more human. My dad looked at the script and was moved by it. I've never done anything for kids and this is going to be great for them. She's tough and real and a warrior, so it's not going to be a cartoon or cute but it has a lot to do about our planet." Jolie has also gone into rigorous physical training for the role. She recently told reporters, "I've been in England for three weeks and we will be there for over a month more just doing training. I'm training throughout the film but it's been great for me. I get up and do yoga at seven in the morning, which is insane! I'm on protein shakes and they've taken my cigarettes and alcohol and sugar away from me—and Billy—because I'm far away." Then Jolie mentioned "bungee ballet . . . diving, [and] weapons training with the Special Forces. I'm doing kickboxing—everything from soccer to rowing. I've got to get my British accent down, and one British thing is to learn manners. Lara was raised with upper-class manners that are broken down, so they're sending me to manners school. I think that's really funny. *Me* in manners class!"

All of these recent interviews are infused with Jolie's trademark humor and boundless energy. She sounds more confident and happy now than she's ever been. Perhaps it's because she's married to the love of her life and for the first time she feels complete. As she said to *Talk* magazine, "My priorities have changed. My life has changed. Today in my life I just feel like the luckiest, most blessed . . . I don't know how to explain it."

Looking to the future, Jolie describes her vision of happiness. With her words she paints a picture that's simple yet very compelling: "You know, we all need to just wake up excited about life. I just want to do the job I always wanted to do since I was a little girl, and live in peace with family and people I love, and just be silly and collect T-shirts from gas stations and go on road trips and eat popcorn in the middle of the night and watch T.V. That's all I want, you know?"

WORKS CITED

(*Note*: In addition to the sources listed below, wire service items, press interviews, and press releases have been used extensively.)

Anderson, Diane. "'Tis the Season to Be Jolie." *Girlfriends* Dec. 1997.

Angeli, Michael. "Tres Jolie." *Movieline* Feb. 1999.

"Angelina in Love." *Talk* June/July 2000.

Archerd, Army. "Just for Variety." *Variety* 17 Jan. 1997.

——. "Just for Variety." *Variety* 25 Feb. 1997.

——. "Just for Variety." *Variety* 2 July 1998.

Ascher-Walsh, Rebecca, et al. "Fall Movie Preview: October." *Entertainment Weekly* 22 Aug. 1997.

Atkinson, Michael. Rev. of *Hell's Kitchen*. 1999. www.mrshowbiz.com

Avins, Mimi. "A Sleeping Beauty: Gia Carangi Had It All, Or So It Seemed in the *Cosmo* Cover Photos of Her." *Los Angeles Times* 29 Jan. 1998.

Bark, Ed. "Race to the Finish: Sinise Cements Wallace's Place in History." *Dallas Morning News* 23 Aug. 1997.

Barnes, Harper. "Tripping on the Net: Sophomoric Is the Sum of It." *St. Louis Post-Dispatch* 15 Sept. 1995.

Berardinelli, James. "*Foxfire*: A Film Review." 1996. http://movie-reviews.colossus.net/movies

Bergman, Anne. "A Proverbial Adventurer." *Los Angeles Times* 17 Nov. 1999.

Berlin, Joey. "Actor Stewart Loves New Role: Romance Blooms in *Heart*." *Washington Times* 13 Jan. 1999.

Bernstein, Paula S. "*Love Is All There Is*: Oft-Told Tale Is Truly a Tragedy." 1996. *New Jersey Star Ledger*. www.njo.com

Boleyn, Alison. "Celebrity Profile: Angelina Jolie." *Marie Claire* Feb. 2000.

Braun, Liz. "Billy Bob Thornton Gets His Jolies." *Ottawa Sun* 26 June 2000.

D'Souza, Christa. "Do You Wanna Be in My Gang? Actor Jonny Lee Miller Is Mr. Cool." *Daily Telegraph* 17 Mar. 2000.

Daly, Steve, et al. "Spring Movie Preview: The A List." *Entertainment Weekly* 12 Feb. 1999.

Dawson, Angela. "Angelina Jolie: Revving Her Engines." *Newsday* 13 June 2000.

——. "Angelina Jolie Running in Fast Lane." *Arizona Republic* 11 June 2000.

"Decisions, Decisions, Decisions: Interview with Jonny Lee Miller." Mar. 1999. http://members.tripod.com/~Odessa-x/interviews.html

Deitch Rohrer, Trish. "Dangerous Beauties: Winona Ryder and Angelina Jolie Walk on the Wild Side." *Premiere* Oct. 1999.

Denerstein, Robert. "*Playing God* Isn't Much Fun (For Anyone)." *Denver Rocky Mountain News* 17 Oct 1997.

Dretzka, Gary. "Angelina Jolie Warily Regards Rising Fame." *Chicago Tribune* 4 Sept. 1996.

Edel, Raymond A. "People." *Record* 15 Apr. 1999.

Essex, Andrew. "Girl Uncorrupted: Razor-Sharp Turns in *Gia* and *Wallace* Got Her Noticed." *Entertainment Weekly* 5 Nov. 1999.

Fisher, Bob. "A Poignant Pas de Deux." *American Cinematographer* Dec. 1998.

Fretts, Bruce. "The Entertainers '99." *Entertainment Weekly* 24 Dec. 1999.

Frey, Darcy. "Something's Got to Give." *New York Times Magazine* 24 Mar. 1996.

Ganahl, Jane. "Actor Laments Curse of the Pretty Boy." *Dallas Morning News* 27 July 1996.

Garner, Jack. "Jolie's Performance in *Playing by Heart* Is Drawing Attention." Gannett News Service 21 Jan. 1999.

Germain, David. "Angelina Jolie Brushes Off Bad Press." *Dallas Morning News* 11 June 2000.

Gilbey, Ryan. "A Cat with Nine Former Lives." *Independent* 2 May 1996.

"Girl, Uninhibited." *Maxim* June 2000.

Gleiberman, Owen. Rev. of *Girl, Interrupted*. *Entertainment Weekly* 7 Jan. 2000.

——. "Up, Up, and Awry: John Cusack and Billy Bob Thornton Fly the Unfriendly Skies." *Entertainment Weekly* 30 Apr. 1999.

Goldman, Steve. "Angelina Jolie." *Total Film* Mar. 2000.

Gorman, Steve. "Update 1: Billy Bob Thornton, Angelina Jolie Marry." Reuters 8 May 2000.

Greppi, Michele. "Gia: Supermodel in the Raw." *New York Post* 31 Jan. 1998.

Gritten, David. "Mr. Unpredictable: *Four Weddings* Director Mike Newell's Latest Film Is Neither Fish Nor Fowl." *Daily Telegraph* 25 Oct. 1999.

Hall, Carla. "A Man and His 'X': Setting Up for a Fifth Season of *The X-Files*." *Los Angeles Times* 26 Oct 1997.

Hardy, Ernest. "*Hell's Kitchen*: No Escape from the Past, Especially a Criminal One." *New York Times* 3 Dec. 1999.

Harrison, Eric. "The Many Faces of Voight . . ." *Los Angeles Times* 22 Jan. 1999.

Heckman, Don. "Jolie Breathes Life into Gia's tragic Tale." *Los Angeles Times* 31 Jan. 1998.

Heisler, Bob. "Talk It Up." *Newsday* 31 Jan. 1999.

Heyman, J.D. "Angelina Jolie Marries Billy Bob Thornton." *Us* 22 Apr. 2000.

Hobson, Louis B. "An Old Soul." *London Free Press* 20 Apr. 1999.

——. "Angie, Committed." *Edmonton Sun* 9 Jan 2000.

——. "Bad Is Good for Voight." *Ottawa Sun* 10 Jan. 1999.

——. "Being Intimate with Sarah." *Ottawa Sun* 6 Sept 1999.

——. "Clean Image Suits Nolte." *Calgary Sun* 14 Dec. 1998.

——. "Dark Angel: Angelina Jolie Collects Knives and Tattoos." *Edmonton Sun* 5 Nov. 1999.

——. "Jolie Intense to the Bone." *Calgary Sun* 31 Oct 1999.

——. "Pieces of Heart Form Incomplete Picture." *London Free Press* 22 Jan. 1999. Nov. 1999.

——. "Princely Phillipe: Hot Hollywood Actor Is Playing by Heart on the Screen and in Real Life." *Edmonton Sun* 25 Jan. 1999.

——. "Pushing Her Luck: Angelina Jolie's Full-Tilt Existence." *Calgary Sun* 18 Apr. 1999.

——. "Shooting Stars: The Hot Faces of Tomorrow." *Calgary Sun* 1 Jan. 1999.

Holt, Jessica. "Ryder Discusses Personal Meaning of *Girl, Interrupted*." *University Wire* 10 Jan. 2000.

"In the Spotlight: Double Dipping Newcomer Elizabeth Mitchell Pops in *Frequency* and as Linda McCartney on T.V." *People* 22 May 2000.

Interview with Angelina Jolie. 23 May 2000. www.beatboxbetty.com

Interview with Angelina Jolie. 11 June 2000. www.beatboxbetty.com

Interview with Jonny Lee Miller. *Just 17*. http://members.tripod.com/~Odessa-X/just17.html

Ivry, Bob. "A Man and His Times." *Record* 24 Aug. 1997.

——. "Relatively Secret." *Record* 25 Apr. 1999.

James, Christine. "'Dancing' Queen Angelina Jolie Gets Constructive in *Dancing About Architecture*." www.boxoffice.com

Jenny Shimizu: From Grease Monkey to Supermodel." *Curve* Sept. 1996.

Jewel, Dan, and Deanna Kizis. "Quick Study: For Summer Star Mekhi Phifer, Acting Is a Breeze." *People* 23 Nov. 1998.

Johnson, G. Allen. "Duchovny Outshines Rest at *Playing God*." *San Francisco Examiner* 17 Oct. 1997.

"Jonny Lee Miller and Angelina Jolie: The Happy Couple." *Empire* June 1996.

Jucaud, Dany. "And the Devil Created Angelina Jolie." *Paris Match* 17 Feb. 2000.

Kaplan, James. "Holy Moly, It's Angelina Jolie." *Allure* Mar. 1999.

Kelleher, Terry, and John Griffiths. "Picks and Pans: Tube." *People* 25 Aug. 1997.

Kennedy, John F., Junior. Interview with George Wallace. *George* Oct./Nov. 1995.

Kenny, Glenn, et al. "Video: The Week." *Entertainment Weekly* 23 Feb. 1996.

King, Susan. "Don't Hate Her Because She's Lucky." *Los Angeles Times* 24 Aug. 1996.

——. "Runaway Actor: After a Lengthy Quiet Period, Jon Voight Is Back." *Los Angeles Times* 20 Nov. 1997.

Kizis, Deanna. "Truth and Consequences." *Harper's Bazaar* Nov. 1999.

——. "What the Hell Is Wrong with Angelina Jolie?' *Jane* Feb. 2000.

Kuklenski, Valerie. "Movie Puts Gia's Life into Perspective." *St. Louis Post-Dispatch* 31 Jan. 1998.

Lanie, Tricia. "Girl Talk: Hollywood's Actresses Are Abuzz About the Film Version of *Girl, Interrupted*." *Entertainment Weekly* 23 Oct. 1998.

Late Night with Conan O'Brien. NBC. 29 Jan. 1998.

Laura Dern Isn't the Only One Who's Less than Thrilled with Angelina Jolie's New 'Billy Bob' Tattoo." *Daily Telegraph* 27 Apr. 2000.

Levy, Maury Z. "Cover Girl." *Philadelphia* Jan.1980.

Longsdorf, Amy. "Angelina Jolie as the Ill-Fated Supermodel in the Biopic *Gia*." *Playboy* May 2000.

——. "Sean Connery Feeling Independent in His Latest Movie." Gannett News Service 26 Jan. 1999.

Mackenzie, Drew, and Ivor Davis. "I'm Both Sinister and Soft." *Woman's Day* (Australia) 17 Apr. 2000.

Mann, Barry. "I Have No One to Have Sex With." *NW* 24 Jan. 2000.

Mansfield, Stephanie. "I'm Appreciating Life, Seeing the Possibilities." *USA Weekend* 11 June 2000.

——. "Oscar-Winning Actress Angelina Jolie Says She's Putting Her Wild Past Behind Her." *USA Weekend* 11 June 2000.

Marder, Diana. Knight Ridder Newspapers 30 Jan. 1998.

Martin, Ed. "Gutsy *Gia* Goes Beyond Skin Deep." *USA Today* 30 Jan. 1998.

Mathews, Jack. "Don't Quit Your Day Job, David." *Newsday* 17 Oct. 1997.

——. "A Sitcom Parody of the Star-Crossed Lovers." *Newsday* 14 Oct. 1996.

Miller, Prairie. "A *Simple Plan*: Interview with Billy Bob Thornton." *Star Interviews* 1 Jan. 1998.

——. "Interview with Jon Voight." *Star Interviews* 1 Jan. 1998.

——. "*Playing by Heart*: Interview with John Stewart." *Star Interviews* 8 Mar. 1999.

Nash, Alanna. "Gia: Fashion Victim." *Entertainment Weekly* 16 Jan. 1998.

——. "The Model Who Invented Heroine Chic." *New York Times* 7 Sept. 1997.

News Extra. 19 Jan. 1990, Montreal, QC, Canada. http://www.konni.com/angelina.nsf/pages/article1.html

Nicholson, William F. "'Terrible Lawyer' Keeps Wheels of Justice Turning." *USA Today* 13 Aug. 1998.

Norris, Chris. "Say Goodbye to the Brooding Gen-Xer: Winona Ryder Has Grown into a Woman of Impeccable Taste." *In Style* 2 Jan. 2000.

"Now Our Mel's Starring in the Crying Game." *Sunday Mail* 27 Feb. 2000.

Oates, Joyce Carol. Introduction. *Foxfire: Confessions of a Girl Gang.* New York: Dutton, 1993.

"On the Move: Name Dropper Not Billing Herself as a Voight." *People* 8 July 1996.

Osborne, Bert. Interview with Angelina Jolie. *Jezebel* Feb. 2000.

Parks, Steve. "Flawed Minis Are Still Worth Watching." *Newsday* 18 May 1997.

Parnes, Francine. "The Sweet Face of the Future." *Daily Telegraph* 26 May 1999.

Pearlman, Cindy. "A Jolie Good Time." *Daily Telegraph.* 10 June 2000.

Pevere, Geoff. "Boys Will Be Boys, But Then So Will Men." *Toronto Star* 23 Apr. 1999.

——. "*Girl* an Unsatisfying Minor Interruption." *Toronto Star* 21 Dec. 1999.

Pinsker, Beth. "*Foxfire* Extinguishes Oates Novel's Spark." *Dallas Morning News* 26 Aug. 1996.

"*Plunkett and Macleane*: Interview with Jonny Lee Miller." http://members.tripod.com/~Odessa-X/interviews.html

Pond, Steve, and Renee Vogel. "Hollywood Now: Class of '98, The Kids Are All Right." *Los Angeles Times* 22 Mar. 1998.

Profumo, Tony. "In Brando's League." *Los Angeles Times* 14 Nov. 1999.

Ressner, Jeffrey. "Rebel Without a Pause." *Time* 24 Jan. 2000.

Richardson, John H. "Angelina Jolie and the Torture of Fame." *Esquire* Feb. 2000.

Richmond, Ray. Rev. of *Gia. Variety* 28 Jan. 1998.

Rohan, Virginia. "Wallace Agonistes." *Record* 18 Aug. 1997.

Roush, Matt. "Crass Self-Destruction: Heroic Tale of *True Women*." *USA Today* 16 May 1997.

Rozen, Leah, Tom Cunneff, and Tom Gliatto. "Picks and Pans: Screen." *People* 15 Nov. 1999.

Sandell, Laurie. "Reckless Angel." *Biography* Oct 1999.

Saunders, Dusty. "*True Women*: True Frontier Grit." *Denver Rocky Mountain News* 18 May 1997.

Scaduto, Anthony. "Flash! The Latest Entertainment News and More." *Newsday* 4 Sept 1996.

Scavullo, Francesco. *Scavullo: Photographs, 50 Years.* New York: Abrams: 1997.

——. *Scavullo Women.* New York: Harper and Row, 1982.

Schwarzbaum, Lisa. "The Odd Couples: Romantic Entanglements and Family Strife Beat at the Center of *Playing by Heart*." *Entertainment Weekly* 22 Jan. 1999.

Seiler, Andy. "Heart: Relationships with No Short Cuts." *USA Today* 22 Jan. 1999.

Seymour, Gene. "Disorder in the Ward: A Memoir of a Teen Mental Institution." *Newsday* 21 Dec. 1999.

Shapiro, Erik. Letter to the Editor. *Entertainment Weekly* 26 Nov. 1999.

Simon, Brent. "Girl, Conflicted." *Entertainment Today* Jan. 2000.

Slotek, Jim. "Voight Praises New Players; *Varsity Blues* 'Coach' Relishes Working with the Next Generation of Stars." *Toronto Sun* 29 Jan. 1999.

Smith, Liz. "The New Courtney." *Newsday* 24 Aug. 1997.

Snead, Elizabeth. "*Gia* Taps Angelina Jolie's Wild Side." *USA Today* 29 Jan. 1998.

——. "Jolie Embraces Love, Fame for More than 60 Seconds." *USA Today* 8 June 2000.

——. "These Sibs Are Close, But Not That Close!" *USA Today* 7 Apr. 2000.

Spicer, Kate. "Stand and Deliver, It's Jonny Lee Miller." *Minx* Apr. 1998.

Stenze, Jack. "Get Reel: Can Angelina Jolie Make Lara Croft Soar on Screen?" *Entertainment Weekly* 14 Apr. 2000.

Stevenson, Peter M. "Venus Rising." *Mirabella* Jan. 1999.

Stoynoff, Natasha. "She's Having a Jolie Time Kissing." *Toronto Sun* 18 June 2000.

Strickler, Jeff. "Actors Hope They Can Hack It: Cyber-Film Stars Faked Computer Skills." *Minneapolis Star Tribune* 10 Sept. 1995.

Sumner, Jane. "Bringing Story to Film Took Pioneer-Style Determination." *Dallas Morning News* 18 May 1997.

——. "Fittingly, T.V. Film Has Woman's Touch." *Dallas Morning News* 9 May 1997.

——. "'True' Romance: Texas Settings of Historical Novel Attract Tourists, Viewers." *Dallas Morning News* 18 May 1997.

Susman, Gary. Rev. of *Foxfire*. 1996. www.roughcut.com

Sutton, Larry, Ken Baker, and Champ Clark. "Ark de Triumph: Jon Voight Sets Sail on T.V. as Noah." *People* 3 May 1999.

Tatara, Paul. "Duchovny, Hutton Fail Miserably at *Playing God*." CNN. 22 Oct 1997.

Te Koha, Nui. "Hot Joy Ride for Jolie." *Advertiser* 29 June 2000.

——. "Psychiatric Ward Stay No 'Jolie' Matter." *Sunday Mail* 21 May 2000.

The Fifty Most Beautiful People in the World, 1998." *People* 11 May 1998.

Thompson, Bob. "Johnny Be Good: Actor, Writer and Producer Cusack Is Still Learning." *Edmonton Sun* 20 Apr. 1999.

Thompson, David. "Drive Us Wild, Angelina." *Salon* 14 June 2000.

Thompson, Bob. "The Many Faces of Angelina." *Toronto Sun* 11 Apr. 1999.

Today. NBC. 23 Oct.1997.

Tonight Show. NBC. 29 Jan. 1998.

Udovitch, Mimi. "The Devil in Miss Jolie." *Rolling Stone* 19 Aug. 1999.

——. "Women We Love: Angelina Jolie." *Esquire* Feb. 1998.

Van Gelder, Lawrence. Rev. of *Hell's Kitchen.* 1999. www.film.com

Vognar, Chris. "Flawed Execution Mars Noble Aims." *Dallas Morning News* 18 May 1997.

——. "On the Edge: Story of a Young Woman's Breakdown Is Both Dark and Illuminating." *Dallas Morning News* 14 Jan. 2000.

Voight, Jon. "Angelina Jolie." *Interview* June 1977.

Weiner, Sherry. Interview with Angelina Jolie. 1999. www.univercity.com

Williams, Jeannie. "Connery Prim on Matters of the Heart." *USA Today* 22 Jan. 1999.

——. "'Fair' Game After Oscar Party." *USA Today* 28 Mar. 2000.

——. "Voight a Dad Close to His Own 'Babies.'" *USA Today* 12 Mar. 1999.

Williamson, Kim. Rev. of *Love Is All There Is.* 1996. www.boxoffice.com

Wilson, Jeff. "More Special Effects, More Movie Accidents." *Newsday* 23 Dec. 1992.

Wire Service Roundup, 10 June 1999. *Movieline.* www.people.com

Wire Service Roundup, 10 June 1999. *New York Post.* www.people.com

Wloszczyna, Susan, Andy Seiler, and David Patrick Stearns. "Cate the Great Makes Move from Monarch to Mall Queen." *USA Today* 16 Apr. 1999.

Wong, Martin. Rev. of *Foxfire.* A. *Magazine* 30 Sept. 1996.

Wuntch, Phillip. "*The Bone Collector*: Villain Doesn't Have a Spine." *Dallas Morning News* 11 May 1999.

Zacharek, Stephanie. Rev. of *Pushing Tin. salon.com* 23 Apr. 1999.